MIRROR OF MY PAST

MIRROR OF MY PAST

Reflections of a Filipina
After Immigrating to America

Melba Avenido Speer

Library of Congress Control Number: 2007905592
ISBN: Hardcover   978-1-4257-7902-3
               Softcover   978-1-4257-7839-2

To order additional copies of this book, contact:
Xlibris Corporation
1-888-795-4274
www.Xlibris.com
Orders@Xlibris.com
32401

CONTENTS

CONTENTS

Acknowledgments

I would like to thank my husband, Lonnie, for his encouragement to complete this project and for his help in editing the work, to all of the Americans who I came into contact with when I first arrived who showed me such friendliness and encouragement, Glen and the late Betty Speer, who were the first of my husband's relatives I met on my arrival to America and who showed me so much kindness, love, care and understanding when I first arrived, Randy and Merlinda Speer who were the second set of relatives I met who were so friendly and caring and to so many, many others I met along the way.

The Legend of Malakas and Maganda

In the beginning there was only the vast nothingness of the universe.

In His loneliness the supreme God created the world.

One day, the sea-eagle god Manaul alit on a bamboo tree.

Hearing knocking in the bamboo, Manaul pecked on it
until it split and revealed a handsome man who
called himself Malakas (strong).

Malakas then asked Manaul to peck at another bamboo.

When it too split it revealed a woman, Maghanda (beautiful).

Manaul then took the couple to a beautiful island in the East
where they started the brown race.

An old Philippine folk tale

Prologue

It is said that the Philippine Islands was "discovered" by Ferdinand Magellan in 1521 and was named in honor of King Philip of Spain. The truth is, what would eventually become known as the Philippine Islands was never "discovered" by anyone. The islands had been in existence since the dawn of time, rising from the ocean floor during eons of volcanic activity.

If anything, the "discovery of the *existence* of people on the islands" MIGHT be attributed to the Malaysians and Chinese who had been trading with them for over a century before Magellan ever arrived. The Malays, it is believed, had originally migrated over and peopled the islands and had done so, based on archaeological evidence, sometime around 15,000 B.C. By Magellan's time, these inhabitants referred to themselves as Tagalos—people of, basically, a Malayo-Polynesian mix. What happened after Magellan and the first Europeans arrived, however, would go on to dramatically influence the history of the islands and its people.[1]

Magellan chanced upon the area during his circumnavigation of the world and piloted his ships into the interior of the archipelagos seeking a site to replenish his supplies and to refresh his crew. Dropping anchor off the coast of a large inner island called Zzubu (present-day Cebu), he exchanged gifts for food with the island's *datu* (ruling chief) and over the following days convinced the *datu* and his *reyna* (queen) that they should convert to Magellan's religion of Catholicism in order to remain close friends in peace. They consented and soon afterwards Raja Humabon, his wife Queen Juana, and their immediate family, were all baptized. Magellan then went on to insist that ALL inhabitants of the island, including the rest of their relatives and the other clan chieftains and their families should convert. Humabon and his Queen agreed to allow Magellan and his chaplain, Father Pedro Valderrama, to hold a large public baptism ceremony on April 14, 1521, at the location of what is now downtown Cebu City. Humabon's nephew and heir-Prince Raja Cilumai, and his immediate family, as well as a number of other clan chieftains and their families, were all baptized by the chaplain as Magellan and his crew watched. "[W]e baptized eight hundred persons [including] men, women, and children," marveled Antonio Pigafetta, one of Magellan's crewmen who kept a journal of the voyage. Afterwards, Magellan had his men erect a large wood cross at the site to mark the location of the all-important ceremony.[2]

In the following days, Magellan demanded that all clan lords throughout the area, their families, and all of their subjects burn their pagan idols, convert to his religion, and believe in Jesus Christ. He then threatened death to any of those who refused and burned several so-called "disobedient" villages in the vicinity to make his point. At the same time, Magellan demanded that all local tribes pledge their allegiance to Raja Humabon who was to serve as Magellan's surrogate and represent the crown of Spain in his absence. Within five days, nearly all of the inhabitants of Zzubu, estimated at somewhere between 2,000 to 3,000 people, had been converted to the Catholic faith.

On the afternoon of April 26, Lord Zzula of the small, neighboring island of Mattan (now known as Mactan Island), sent a messenger to Zzubu city advising Magellan and *datu* Humabon that he wished to declare his allegiance to them but had been prevented from doing so by the island's overlord, Cacique Cilapulapu.

Chief Lapu-Lapu, as he was more commonly known, was not as easily persuaded as the others by all the demands of the Europeans. He refused to become subservient to the foreigners and had stayed away from all of the previous ceremonies. Zzula asked for help in overthrowing Lapu-Lapu and Magellan decided at once to make an example of this "defiant pagan chief." Against the advise of his officers and that of Humabon, Magellan sent word back with Zzula's messenger not to worry and his warriors would not be needed. Lapu-Lapu, he advised Zzula, would be taken care of by the powerful Europeans, and in short order![3]

By midnight, Magellan headed out toward Mactan Island with three landing boats carrying artillery and 60 men in full armor. King Humabon had offered 1,000 of his best warriors to assist but Magellan had refused this offer too. Arriving at the northwest tip of the island, Magellan sent an emissary ashore to persuade Lapu-Lapu to give up or he and his followers were facing certain death at the hands of the Europeans. The mediator returned with Lapu-Lapu's final reply, which was in essence: "*Onsa pay imong gipa abot? Ali!*" (Cebuano meaning "So what are you waiting for? Come on!")

Infuriated, Magellan immediately ordered his men out of the boats to attack. Because they had arrived at Mactan Island at low tide, the exposed rock and coral surrounding the island made it necessary for the Spaniards to anchor their landing craft 150 to 200 yards from the beach and to wade to shore. They removed and left their lower leg armor in the boats in order to wade through the salt water toward the beach. As the men approached the shore, they found no one in sight but saw three parallel, shallow trenches dug into the white sand—an obstacle difficult for men in armor to cross quickly. As the soldiers walked across the short stretch of sand and approached the first trench, the silence was broken by a loud jeering crowd emerging from a line of palms boarding the backside of the beach.[4]

"[W]e found fifteen hundred of the islanders divided into three [groups]," wrote Antonio Pigafetta, who was himself wounded in the highly pitched battle that was to ensue, "of which one opposed our advance while the others assailed us on the flanks."[5]

As the jeering crowd of islanders rushed down onto the beach toward the soldiers, Magellan marshaled his men into two defensive groups and, because the trenches presented an obstacle to his men, had them take several steps back into the surf and form a wedge-shaped formation. The bombards back in the boats immediately opened fire but because of their distance from the shore, they had little affect.

At first the Tagalo warriors were startled by the noise of the gunfire, but when they saw it had no effect, they rushed the Spaniards in a classic sweeping-crescent maneuver, the center engaging the enemy as the sides swung in for double envelopment. Within moments they had outflanked the Spanish soldiers, absorbing their small arms and crossbow fire.[6]

"Shouting more and more loudly and jumping from side to side to disconcert our aim," Pigafetta continued, "they advance simultaneously [and] we were scarcely able to defend ourselves."[7]

Once close enough, the warriors, many carrying a simple shield of woven bamboo slats, unleashed a barrage of rocks and arrows as well as bamboo lances, which Pigafetta described as some being "tipped with iron," and others being "pointed stakes hardened by fire."

Such weapons had little effect on the Spanish armor, though, until one lance happened to penetrate the lower leg of a soldier. After that, the Tagalos concentrated their attack on their enemy's lower legs, where the armor had been removed back at their boats. First one Spaniard fell, then another. Magellan, who was struck by a lance in the face just below his helmet, tried to draw his sword but was prevented by another wound. He then ordered a retreat just as he was wounded a third time and fell face first into the surf. With 19 other armored casualties laying along the beach and in water, the remaining soldiers scrambled for the boats that were already beginning to pull away. Lapu-Lapu, having lost only 15 warriors in the fight, immediately confiscated the Spanish-made swords, halberds, lances, crossbows, and other more advanced weapons as well as the helmets, corselets and 20 suits of armor for future use.

Raja Humabon was saddened by the death of the explorer and the Spanish defeat but quickly realized his predicament Cilapulapu was a great leader with a powerful army long before the Spaniards had arrived. Now, with the Spanish weapons and armor, he would surely be invincible in the region. The Spaniards that had survived the battle insisted that Humabon go to Mactan Island and beg for the return of Magellan's body. Reluctantly, the Raja agreed but later returned, professing that Lapu-Lapu had refused. A few days later, on May 1, Humabon's nephew invited the remaining Spanish officers to a banquet and had them massacred. Those who had remained on the ships saw what was happening on shore, pulled anchor and fled the area, eventually arriving back in Spain to relate the story of Magellan's death.[8]

The people of the island went back to their daily lives without any outside interference for a few years not knowing that the Spanish had already laid their "claim" on the area. Three more Spanish expeditions followed Magellan's, all sailing from Mexico which had since become a Spanish colony. Alonso de SaavedraCeron arrived in 1528 commanding three ships with a total of about 115 crewmen, looking for any survivors of the Magellan expedition. He reached what is probably known today as Lanuza Bay in the province of present-day Surigao del Sur, traded with some of the locals and apparently reconnoitered the development of the current state of their weapons of war, describing them as being long arrows and blowguns tipped with poisoned herbs, iron cutlasses, cannons, and that they wore cotton corselets in battle. Although his journals and report survived, Saavedra died in the South Seas before he got back to Mexico. In 1542 Ruy Lopez de Villalobos ventured out from Mexico with six ships and nearly 370 men and landed on the east coast of present-day Mindanao in 1543. At present-day Sarangani Island he ordered his men to plow the land to plant corn—the first on Philippine soil—and intended to set up a colony. Again claiming the area for Spain, he officially named the island nation, *Islas Felipinas*, (Islands of Philip) after King Philip II of Spain. Extreme hunger due to the absence of enough food forced his men to eat all of the available dogs, cats and rats in the region, along with grubs, lizards, and unknown plants and crabs that the locals knew to be poisonous. As the men died and the colony failed, the remaining survivors left Sarangani and Villalobos later succumbed to a malignant fever, never to return to Mexico. Unknown to the islands' inhabitants, however, the Spanish government was making plans to eventually return to revenge Magellan's death, regain control of the area that he and the others had claimed "for the crown," and to colonize the island nation as they had Mexico. After another 22 years had passed, the Spanish returned with a vengeance on April 28, 1565, when a force of conquistadors under Miguel Lopes de Legazpi stormed upon the beaches of Cebu at present-day site of Cebu City, burned the villages and crops there, killed many of the islanders as others fled to the mountains, and ultimately established the first permanent settlement in what would become the Spanish colony of the Philippines. The Spanish went on to rule and influence the Philippines over the following 300 years. In that regard, the country began to develop along the same lines as Mexico. In fact, today there are many similarities between the two countries and their people. They share many words and customs and like Mexico, nearly ninety percent of the island nation is Roman Catholic and remains the only Christian country in Asia. Various struggles for Philippine independence erupted in a number of locations throughout the country between 1872 to 1897 and during this period noted revolutionary Dr. Jose Rizal was executed by the Spanish authorities for such attempts. In 1898, as a result of the Spanish-American War, the United States of America took possession of the Philippines and established it, first, as a commonwealth and then as a U.S. Administration. The U.S. occupation of the Philippines continued, during which time they, too, put down several attempts at Independence, both armed struggles and diplomatic attempts, over the following years. With Japan's attack on the U.S. Naval fleet at Pearl Harbor on December 7, 1941, U.S. military installations in Manila, Philippines, was attacked at the same time. Filipino troops fighting along side the Americans suffered comparable casualties and defeats in the following weeks. Many Filipino soldiers died shoulder to shoulder with the American troops during the battle of Bataan and the Bataan Death March that followed. This eventually brought about the brutal Japanese military rule over the Philippines that continued until 1944 when General Douglas MacAuthur fulfilled his promise to return to liberate the nation from the Japanese. Once WWII came to an end, the United States of America finally granted the Philippines full independence on July 4, 1946 and the Republic of the Philippines elected its first President.

Eventually the Philippines developed into an independent nation comprised of 7,107 islands that extend 1,143 miles from north to south in the Pacific, southeast of the Asian continent, 621 miles southeast of the China coast and 7,330 miles west of mainland USA. Only about 2,000 of its islands are inhabited and only 500 are larger than one square kilometer. The country is divided into 72 provinces, 61 chartered cities, and thousands of small towns and communities called barengays. Throughout the island nation there are some 111 linguistic, cultural and racial groups. Although the national language is Filipino based on *Tagalog*—the dialect of the Tagalog people of the Manila and South Luzon region—there is another 70 languages and dialects belonging to the Malayo-Polynesian family of tongues spoken throughout the country. So, in reality, a Filipino from one location might not understand a Filipino from another. Luckily, English is the language of education and commerce in the Philippines. Filipinos are taught English from grade school through high school and college. For the most part, business and business documents are all conducted in English.

As a result of its varied history, Philippine people, cuisine, language, culture, and customs are all a mixture of Malay, Chinese, Spanish, and American. It is often joked that Filipinos are Malay in family, Spanish in love, Chinese in business, and American in ambition; that their culture is a result of over 300 years living in a convent and nearly 50 years living in Hollywood! The current population of the nation is around 71.6 million (1995). In addition to its nearly ninety-percent Roman Catholic, five-percent are Protestant, three-percent are Muslim, and 2-percent are other such as Buddhist or Taoist Chinese, Jehovah's Witness, Mormon, and Seventh-Day Evangelists, etc.

   The early years of independence and the initial development of the country followed along the same lines of rural and small-town America or, in some places Mexico, again because of the country's history and early influence of those people upon the general population. The country continued to do well under its first four or five presidents, through the 1950s and 1960s. It became the leading democratic nation of southeast Asia. Many regional and national conferences were held there. Bicycles, motorcycles, buses, and surplus jeeps left over from the U.S. Army became common modes of travel. Boy Scouts, Girl Scouts, and other clubs and organizations such as the Lion's Clubs and Freemasonry Masonic Lodges sprang up everywhere. In fact, the World Boy Scout Jamboree was held there in 1959 in Makiling National Park. Over these years, tourism proliferated. Baseball and basketball became the most popular community sporting events and, eventually, basketball developed into the country's national sport. The Philippines and its people remained fairly well off and developed quite naturally until 1972 and the mid-Marcos regime. According to my husband—who knows his history—when Ferdinand Marcos was elected the nation's sixth President in 1965 the Philippine Peso (Piso) was valued at two peso to the U.S. dollar. President Marcos and his wife Imelda became the John and Jackie Kennedy of the Philippines. They were a young, vibrant and handsome couple and Imelda was quite attractive. They became very popular and overwhelmingly adored by the general populace. They were seen everywhere together although Imelda often visited other countries as a popular good-will ambassador for her husband. She preferred the title of First Lady, emulating the Americans, and they seemed to do everything in the sole interest of their country and its people. In fact, they brought many cultural and technological advances to the Philippines such as improving rice productivity by introducing the IR8 "miracle rice" hybrid variety and promoted many other innovations that improved public health and nutrition. Ferdinand Marcos was overwhelmingly re-elected in 1969—the first Filipino President ever re-elected. But as they say, "power corrupts," and he and the First Lady apparently fell under its spell. Facing the conclusion of his second and final term, Marcos declared martial-law on September 21, 1972 while convincing the American government that communists were plotting to overthrow the country and that only he could keep the communists from taking over. The Americans were already deeply involved battling communists in Viet Nam and holding them at bay in Korea. They wanted no other Asian country to fall under its spell so they supported President Marcos, both politically and financially. Although Marcos eventually lifted martial law in January of 1981, during the time, he ruled boldly with the American government behind him. He continued his dictatorial form of government with presidential decrees, governing sternly against any political opposition. Meanwhile, he and the First Lady piled up huge foreign debts through lavish spending and amassed a vast personal fortune before being forced out of office in1986. It is estimated that he and Imelda and their political cronies stashed away nearly ten-billion dollars from various corrupt activities over the years before Ferdinand and Imelda finally fled into exile, again aided by the U.S. government, to Hawaii. The Philippine economy and the country has never recovered and, in fact, has been going downhill ever since. It now takes over 40 Philippine peso to buy one American-dollar.[9]

Chief crops of the nation are rice, coconuts and its by-products, pineapples, sugar cane, and corn. Its main industries include fishing, farming, food processing, clothing and textile manufacturing, aqua-culture, furniture manufacturing and micro-electronics. The average income on the islands is around P9,516 per month (about $190 US) or P114,192 per year (or about $2,284 US). Many, of course, make much less. The average Filipino requires about P12,000 per month ($300 US) to meet the basic necessity expenses which is about P144,000 per year or about $3,600 U.S.

Filipino cuisine is a diverse mixture of east and west because of the Malay, Chinese, Spanish, and American influences. Dishes that Americans would be familiar with include spring rolls—containing ground pork, shrimp and cabbage—which exhibit the Chinese influence of the egg roll, as well as a wide variety of egg-noodle and rice dishes. Filipinos eat rice with all three meals of the day much like Americans eat potatoes. While an American thinks nothing of eating hash-browns during breakfast, french fries during lunch and mashed or baked potatoes for supper, a Filipino fixes rice in various ways for each of their meals. The Spanish influence in the Filipino culinary fare can be see in the wide range of hot peppers used in seasoning and the use of tortillas and beans in various dishes. The Malay-Polynesian influence is recognized in the frequent preparations of *lechon*, or roasted pig—served full-form and sometimes with a big red apple in its mouth—with crisp brown skin and tender meat as a result of being basted on a turning spit for hours. The American influences can be seen in the popularity of barbecue, hot-dogs, corn and potato chips, ice cream, and various other fast food and "junk foods," deserts, candy, and other delights. Of course, the Filipino influence developed on its own over time utilizing the wide range of fresh vegetables, fruits, and coconuts that grow on the islands and the nearly unlimited variety of seafood harvested all along its coasts.[10]

The climate of the islands is typically tropical: hot and humid year around averaging 85-degrees Fahrenheit during the day and 75 at night. The country's geology consists mostly of beaches and mountains with narrow stretches of flat land between. There are 37 known volcanos in the Philippines, 17 are active and 20 are inactive. On the average, 20 typhoons, similar to the hurricanes in the United States but rotating in the opposite direction, occur in the area of the Philippines each year. Of that number, an average of nine hit the Philippines directly. A fortunate aspect about the Cebu-Mactan Island area is that there are no active volcanoes there, it is an inner island not in the typical typhoon belt and it is not in an earthquake zone. Still, it does occasionally suffer to one degree or another from those events.[11]

In its relationship with America, people of the Philippines have been migrating to that country since the beginning of its history, too. The first documented arrival of a Filipino into what would be the continental United. States was on October 18, 1587, when a group of Luzon Filipinos, referred to as Luzon Indos at the time, from the Spanish ship *Nuestra Senora de Esperanza* came ashore with a Spanish landing party in the region of what would eventually become known as Morro Bay in the state of California. The first recorded settlement of Filipinos in America was in the mid-1760s, in the St. Malo area along Barataria Bay, just south of New Orleans. The region, originally under French domination, existed at that time as a part of the Spanish territory called West Florida. In 1763 a Filipino crewman originally from Cebu, Philippines, who had been impressed into service on the Spanish galleon, *San Pablo*, jumped ship and fled into the bayous and marshland there. His name is lost to history too but other documentation shows that he was just one of a number of Filipinos who eventually escaped from such ships while anchored in the New Orleans region and settled in the area. These Spanish-speaking Filipinos, more commonly referred to at the time as "Manila-men," are considered the first Asian immigrants to settle in what was to become the continental United States. In fact, because of the extensive Manila galleon trade going on between Mexico and the Philippines between 1556 to 1815, Filipinos are regarded as the earliest Asians to have crossed the Pacific Ocean, or South Seas as it was called back then, to arrive on the North American continent. The population of St. Malo, for many years commonly referred to as Manila Village, grew to 300 to 400 people. It was this Filipino community that developed the remarkable (for many years) innovative process of sun-drying Louisiana shrimp for export to Canada, Asia, and other parts of the world. Although documentation is lacking for the number of Filipinos who might have fought in the American Revolution, records in the National Archives do show that at least 33 Filipinos fought in the American Civil War. Other Philippine influences on American history include such things as the "manila" envelope commonly used since the 1800s and the yo-yo. The manila envelopes were originally made of coarse yellow-brown paper called Manila paper made in the Philippines from Manila hemp or *abaca*. Abaca is a plant native to the country, especially in the Luzon area, and its fibers are used for a wide variety of products including textiles, rope and paper. Such envelopes were found to be superior to those manufactured in the United States at the time and were brought into America for use in business and commerce. The yo-yo was actually an early weapon used in the Philippines that was developed into a toy used by the children there. Pedro Flores, originally from Vintarilocos Norte, Philippines, came to America in 1915 and eventually settled in Santa Barbara, California. He developed the yo-yo as a children's toy for Americans and formed the Flores Yo-yo Corporation. Eventually he had three factories employing more than 600 workers making over 100,000 yo-yos a day. In the 1930s he sold the business to Donald Duncan who went on to develop the famous Duncan Yo-Yo Company. There are many, many other examples of the Philippine influence on American life as there is American influence on Filipino life.[12]

Today there are over two-million Filipinos in the United States, the second largest group of Asians in America—second only to the Chinese. In addition, records compiled by the U.S. Immigration and Naturalization Service show that a total of 53,535 Filipinos immigrated to the United States during the period of the 1970s to 1980s, alone. That total number ranks third among the many nations from which most U.S. immigrants have been admitted during the past two decades—preceded only by Mexico and mainland China.[13]

Out of forced economic migration, one of every ten Filipinos leave the Islands to work overseas in order to help provide their family a better life. Such people are considered *Bayani* (heros) in my country. They risk their lives and safety to go to a far-off land to provide for their family. In effect, I became one of them. One who is willing to put away their fear, go to a different country to seek a better life, to dream, to help their family, and to experience what it is really like to live in a foreign land, among foreign people. No matter how dangerous it might be it didn't stop me to have such dreams. I wanted a better life. I wanted to help my family. And I wanted to impress my mother so that she would see me in a different way. In my thoughts, I didn't have anything to loose but my life and who would *really* care. I wasn't scared so much in losing my life because I had learned nothing lasts forever. Throughout my life I had lost so many people that I had cared for, young and old, alike—Aunts, Uncles, cousins, friends—and for a variety of reasons—disease, illness, accidents, and a wide range of weather and nature-related catastrophes.

Although all of this history might not seem important now, it has formed the background of my life and eventually, out of it, came my present-day existence. It is who I am. My foundation. My beginning.

CHAPTER 1

Growing Up in the Philippines

I grew up in the community of Gun-ob, Timpolok in the town of Lapu-Lapu City, Cebu Philippines. Lapu-Lapu, or *Opon* as the old folks referred to it, is a little resort town located on Mactan Island in the province of Cebu in the south-central part of the country. The town is located just over the large 900-meter bridge from Cebu City, the country's third largest urban center.[1]

While I was very young I remember that my parents transferred our little Nipa hut from one location to another many times. That was because we did not own any land. We owned our house but we didn't have any property. According to my father, the first house that the family had was located near the fish pond where he worked. I didn't exist then nor did any of my sisters or brothers. According to papa, it was a little shelter constructed mostly of coconut materials. It wasn't a fancy house but it served its purpose. It was good shelter to hide in when the sun shined brightly or when the rain fell heavily. Then when my oldest sister was born they built their second house. It, too, was a small Nipa hut but it was a little bit nicer and a little bit stronger than the first and it was located next to my grandparent's big house, on the left side of it, close to the street. A Nipa hut, or *bahay-kubo* as we called it, is a small native Filipino house having a light frame constructed of coconut timber, flooring made of bamboo slats spaced out for good ventilation, walls of woven coconut leaf matting, and a thatched roof made from Nipa palm leaves. The house is normally elevated on stilts from one to five feet above the ground to prevent dampness and flooding from heavy rains and to help prevent rodents and other creatures from entering. In this location we also stored our fuel, pieces of wood that we collect or find, for our cooking. This little house was not really good compared to the neighbors' houses but because of the greenery provided by plants all around it and the very clean environment as a result of my mother's hard work and cleanliness, the house looked wonderful and the variety of colors from the orchids planted all around gave it a simple charm and beauty. This was the house where all six of us children grew up. We spent most of our time next door, in my grandparents larger house, which also had an attached garage for their motorcycle and a store. These were my mother's parents, Floro and Eutropia Tumulak. My father's mother, Gregoria Avenido, who we only saw at Christmas or on special occasions, lived in the mountains near Badian, almost 80 kilometers (or nearly 50 miles) southwest of Lapu-Lapu.

A typical *bahay-kubo* or Nipa hut

My maternal grandparents' place was a big wide, concrete and wood, two-story house of Spanish-influenced architecture painted light green and surrounded by coconut trees, a number of star-fruit trees, several banana trees, and numerous tropical flowering plants and bushes—the names for which I never knew. As a child, the most unforgettable aspect about this big old house was the long, ornate bannister that stretched along the staircase from the first floor to the upstairs. All of the grandchildren were constantly on the stairs climbing up on the bannister to slide down to the ground level. Having no amusement parks, it was the most exciting ride any of us could ever expect to experience. Of course there was the occasional accident on these stairs as a result. I had many cousins who were hurt when they fell from the bannister or tumbled down these stairs over the years. I also remember that the living room floors in this downstairs area were all a deep red highly polished marble that was so shinny we kids could all see our reflections in it. Whenever Lola, Lolo, or our parents were nowhere near, we kids would get a running start and slide across the floor on our knees, backs or bellies to help shine the floors even more.[2] Of course this too sometimes resulted in injuries when we hit the floor wrong and banged our head on the marble as we flopped down to slide and we often left Lola's house with big knots on our heads or dark bruises, looking like a bunch of little bananas. The floors of the upstairs were a highly-shined thick dark mahogany wood that was also so dark and shinny that we could see ourselves. But after a few kids tried to slide on those and caught a big sliver of wood or splinters, all attempts to help shine those floors soon stopped.

At the time, the house was considered one of the oldest and biggest in the Timpolok section of town. My grandparents were deeply established, well-known long-time residents who were greatly thought of in the community. With time, though, the once great house had become old and fell into disrepair. Part of the reason was because Grandpa had grown blind by his early forties and grandmother depended on him too much to initiate any repairs, herself. Then, too, their children had all grown up, married, and moved away, having their own obligations and places to care for and increasingly became unable to help properly take care of the place. I remember that as I was growing up the wood walls and ceilings were already in a state of decay. Because of that, it seemed that many different kinds of creatures lived in the ceilings and the walls of the house from the bottom to the top. Creatures such as rats were the biggest problem but there was also lizards of all sizes and a few birds that made nests both inside and outside the house. These creatures attracted and held the attention of me and my brothers and sisters at all times whenever we were in the house. Every day, just before dark, a big lizard would come out and make a lot of noise. Tu-ko! Tu-ko! Tu-ko! His call would echo all through the old home. I was scared of this big lizard. Every time I entered my grandparents house, I would open my eyes real wide and look all around, carefully watching the ceiling and walls as I focused my hearing and listened closely to all the sounds, hoping the lizard would not jump down on me and sting my skin. I took my parents warning about the danger of this little creature very seriously. They once told me—and it always stuck in my head—that the lizard would never go away once it jumped down on me and stuck into my skin. Nearly a foot long when full grown, these creatures latched onto your skin so tightly they had to be scrapped off. I never knew if their words were true or not but I saw no reason to test them.[3] The scariest part of the house was the upstairs because, even though they were smaller, there was even more lizards living up there and, even worse, *sigben* were there! All of the adults had told me *sigben*—little people like the hobbits or dwarf people which Americans might refer to as boogie men—occupied the ceilings. These little people, I was told, you can not see but they can see you. That is why they warned us children never to go up into the attic area and climb along the ceilings or else we might completely disappear forever. This story was absorbed deeply into my childhood brain. I didn't know if it was true or not at the time but, again, I saw no reason to test them. In fact, for many years I really did believe it, because all the folks in the neighborhood agreed with my parents and grandparents and said it was so. Our aunts and uncles agreed, too, and always told us to obey our parents as well as the eldest brothers or sisters or else we would be subject to being kidnaped by the little people. In the Philippines all the adults—aunts, uncles, and neighbors—take part in the discipline of each other's children. Even all the older brothers and sisters watch out for or control the littler ones. Therefore, as we all run around the neighborhood playing, we are all subject to the discipline of any adult. None of the parents become irritated, jealous, or upset about this. It is accepted. We believe that all of the adults are responsible for raising good citizens in their neighborhood or family. My husband tells me it was once like that in America up into the 1950s.

Another terrifying creature the adults threatened us with was the *Tirong* (tee-rong), a giant creature that people described as being half human and half snake—a devil they said. A number of children had been kidnaped or for some reason had disappeared in this region during one period of my childhood that I remember, and the adults said that those children were probably food of this creature. As we were told during that time, the owner of a big store in Cebu City, Robinson's store, was the keeper of the so-called *Tirong* and that is how they had so much money. They had sold their soul to the Devil in order to be rich but, in return, they had to keep the *Tirong* beneath—or in the basement—of their store for him. In the beginning they had fed it live chickens but as it got bigger, live chickens no longer satisfied its hunger and they were required to provide the *Tirong* with little human children. Of course there was never any proof offered to support this rumor, nor do I know the basis for its reference to the Robinsons but that is what was always being told to us little children during that time.[4]

Another common event for the young children in the Philippines is the care and grooming they receive daily from their mother. As we ran around playing our mother would call us over one at a time to come and sit in her lap, or lie down on the floor, for "head inspection." Mamma would usually do this every afternoon. I really hated this routine because during this time, when the day wasn't quite so hot, kids in the neighborhood would gather in our yard and play all kinds of games. Meanwhile, Mamma would then call me over and I would miss a lot of playtime. It wasn't out of embarrassment of having my head checked. It was because I was missing out on playing. That's the main thing about it that I remember. I wasn't embarrassed by it because none of the other kids thought anything about it. Eventually their mothers would all do the same. It was simply because of the timing of my mamma's routine and, it seemed, my mother did it more often than the other mothers. None of us liked it. My brothers often cried or threw a fit about it and I always fussed with my mother over it. She told me that if I didn't let her check through my hair and remove any lice in it, then the lice would grow and begin to dominate my hair. Then the lice would suck the blood out of my head, just like they did to my Cousin Cecilia—whose family had to shave her head because she had so much lice at the time. As a result, it revealed lots of wounds in her scalp. According to my mother, the lice ate her head. I feared the possibility of becoming like her and having my head shaved. I didn't want the other kids making fun of me like they did her. They had many cruel and awful names for her. The other fear mother instilled in me was that the lice will would take all the nutrients from my body. She used to tell me that she knew I had a good appetite yet she wondered where it all went because I was so short and skinny. So, she said, maybe lice were responsible and if I had a lot of lice and the giant *owak* or hawk-bird found out, it would come down out of the sky and snatch-grab me and take me away. To say the least, I was terrified of *owak* too—at least when I was a kid.

As you can see, lies or fantasy to create fear in the children is used quite often to help discipline the young ones in the Philippines. As I and the other kids got older, though, we grew a little more bolder and a lot less gullible. Then when we rebelled or refused to do as we were told, mamma had to grab us, pinch us, and lead us by our ears to where she had been sitting or spank us all the way over to her chair before we would give up or surrender to her. Sometimes, in a final attempt of rebellion, we would cry so hard—pretending that she had hurt us so the neighbors would hear—that it would embarrass her and she would let us go. Sometimes this trick worked but many times it didn't.

Playing, of course, was the most important event in our little lives. I had few toys growing up. We—my brothers and sisters and cousins—made our toys out of common everyday things or played with what we found. As my little brother, Richein, got older one toy we often made was the "tin-can telephone." We would find two empty cans, make a hole in the one end of each and stretch a string tightly from one can to the other and talk into them. Another toy we would make was to take two tin cans, punch two holes opposite each other in each can and loop a long string through the holes so that we could hold onto them as we stepped up onto the cans and walked down the street on them like little stilts. I got so good with them, in fact, that I could actually run using these tin-can stilts. Most of our games were created or made up by our imagination too, or the older ones passed down the games to us that they used to play. I had an uncle, Uncle Fernando, who often created games for us kids to play. He was always organizing things for us to do. For us girls, he taught us how to play "beauty pageant," a dress-up game we enjoyed very much. Before dark all the kids in the neighborhood, including me and my cousins, would gather in my grandparents front yard to play "Miss Universe." Of course my Uncle Fernando was the coordinator to help make the game a success. Since Grandma had a big house with lots of windows, Uncle Fernando would take down a curtain panel from each window to use as our gowns. He would then tell each of us what to do or what he expected to happen in order for the game to be fun for us and a crowd-pleaser to all the adults watching. For you see, the beauty pageants were not only a joy for us kids but also for all the adults in the neighborhood. All of the parents were proud to have their children showing out and having them taught not to be too shy to sing and dance. During the "Miss Universe" game each girl would choose a country to represent such as Miss USA, Miss Japan, Miss Indonesia, Miss Bangladesh, and so on. Miss Japan seemed to be the easiest country for many of us to say or to remember, so one of us would usually choose that name as quickly as we could. The faster you were, the more you got the name you wanted. Eventually, however, Uncle Fernando began to assign a country's name to us based upon the form of our face, eyes, nose and the color of our skin. As a result, we not only learned geography from our activity but we also learned ethnic characteristics of many people of the world. To this day my husband is amazed at my ability to, more times than not, successfully differentiate the various Asians from a crowd of people by telling him who among them is Filipino, Indonesian, Thai, Japanese, Chinese, Korean, Indian, and so on. It was a great learning experience besides being fun. In those days, in my generation, the girls, from the youngest age on up, all loved the beauty pageant. It was the fad, I guess, of my generation in the Philippines.

Then too, the trees that had been damaged by past typhoons often served as our playground and another essential source for our games. When I was a kid I could climb from tree to tree and felt like I was riding in the air. I moved through the trees like a monkey and I could stand on a little limb and then swing over to another. In my generation the kids loved trees. We all could climb up the big long tall coconut trees and throw the nuts down to someone on the ground. We would shimmy up them quickly and shimmy back down with no fear what so ever and thought nothing of it. It was natural for us. We could climb nearly any tree, especially the fruit trees, like the papaya, mango, guava, star-apple, manzanitas, and guavanos. For one thing, children of the Philippines quickly learn that if you can climb a tree, you have a snack. So, that adds extra incentive. In fact, at a very young age I quickly acquired an ability to recognize and differentiate between the many different fruit trees of the Philippines. I was always on the lookout for fruit trees that had already began to bear fruit! I quickly learned how to recognize when the fruit was ready to harvest. From very early on I had learned from trial and error—grabbing any fruit I saw and taking a bite—as soon as I had become successful getting up into trees. It was probably having a fruit in sight that got me up into that first tree. It created another frightful worry for my mother. She didn't want me climbing way up high into the trees and she didn't want me taking fruit from trees that belonged to our neighbors. I guess I was hungry or maybe I just really loved fruit. I quickly learned that in the early morning before the sun would shine was the best time for me to sneak around to get some fruit from my grandparents tree and from the atis—or custard-apple—tree growing in the yard of our neighbors. I would get up early, pretending to be on my way to the outhouse or aimlessly wander about the yard pulling and throwing grass. As soon as I thought no one was looking at me or paying attention, I would get close enough to the tree to snatch the fruit. Many times, however, I would be startled to find out that not only was I taking the fruit but others were up early in the dark doing it as well! Many mornings I would meet other kids, sometimes my cousins or other neighbors—and sometimes even adults from down the street—all sneaking around like me, snatching the fruit. Some mornings whole groups of us were sneaking around getting in each other's way.

In fact, "raiding" was quite common in many neighborhoods when I was a kid. Whole groups of us would be playing somewhere and someone would bring up the idea of raiding the fruit trees in a nearby yard if they noticed that the owners were not home or had just left while we were playing.

Once the owner was out of sight, we would all run to their fruit trees, many climbing into the tree to retrieve the fruit while others threw rocks to knock it out of the tree. Laughing and giggling as we made our assault, it was like some kind of a "fruit gang" or a bunch of "ruffians" rustling fruit! Our main targets were often the juicy mangos or tamarines in the neighborhood. One of my Uncles also had several sineguelas trees—a deliciously rare fruit extremely high in vitamin-C—that he patiently cultivated in order to sell the fruits in the local markets. Most people in the vicinity who had fruit trees for a commercial operation, usually kept the best specimens for themselves and sold the lessor quality fruits—so they were often our main targets and we would go after the better specimens.

Children of the Philippines adapt to tree climbing quite readily at a young age.

The afternoon was the most popular time of the day for the children, whether after school or during vacation. Kids would gather in the trees to play games like tag. Although we had all kinds of tag games on land and in the water, tag in the trees was probably the most daring. The mango tree was the most used and considered best because of the vastness and flexibility of its branches. Nearly all of its limbs are big and thick but bendable. The mango tree in our neighborhood that we little kids used for our games of tag was one that had been damaged by a typhoon. It also wasn't so tall—its top had been blown out by the storm—or else the game would be too dangerous for us. One person would be "It." Whoever was "It" was responsible to try and "tag" those who play the game. You were not allowed to touch the ground and had to move or swing through the tree to stay away from the tagger—or else you would be the next "It." We also played "horse" in this tree. We would straddle and "ride" the lower branches that were close to the ground and use our feet to help lift or bounce us up high.

As far as having pets to play with, people in the Philippines don't have pets as people do in America. Some very wealthy Filipinos in the big cities such as Cebu City or Manila do have various breeds of dogs that they show off and compete with in dog shows similar to those in America, but for the most part people are too poor in the Philippines to have pets to care for and spend money on. It was surprising to me when I first came to America. It is unheard of and really unbelievable the amount of pampering and luxury that Americans provide their various pets. Dogs and cats in the Philippines are generally stray or feral. Puppies were different. We all loved puppies but once they grew bigger they were often abandoned or had strayed off from their owners who had discovered they were too expensive to keep. We had many street dogs and cats in my neighborhood as I was growing up but we never liked them much. They were mostly scavengers and considered dirty. My fear and hatred of dogs begin when I was very young, maybe age 10 or 11. I was sent out by mama one day to buy a coconut and was attacked by five of them along the way. By the time I was several blocks away from our house a pack of five dogs had surrounded me. I was always small for my age anyway and these dogs were nearly as big as me. They begin their attack, biting my legs and bottom, tearing my dress and T-shirt. I became like a crazy kid, scared, screaming and crying. Luckily, Uncle Dario who drives a motor-trike, happened to be driving by and saw what was happening otherwise I would have been chewed up like bubble gum. Uncle Dario saved me by scaring the dogs off and driving me home. I was in shock and cried and screamed all the way back and he explained to my mother what had happened. And cats, well cats are used so much in movies as devils or witches or always portrayed as being in some way possessed that we really just try to avoid them altogether and I really don't even want to see them. Especially black cats. White hair cats are OK but people in the Philippines remain superstitious, even in this day and age. Still, such animals are a part of daily life in the Philippines. You see them everywhere in town walking around in the neighborhoods looking for food. They eat any food that is dropped on the ground or dumped out with the trash. Even today we will often throw scraps to a stray dog or cat passing by our house but we just have no interest in keeping them as pets.

But, I do remember having a baby goat when I was a little girl that belonged to my uncle Glen. He let us take care of it and when the goat grew bigger and was to be sold, Uncle Glen divided the profits of it with my parents. I grew to love that goat. In fact, it was maybe the first animal friend that I ever had. I took good care of that goat and insisted on finding him a good place where there was plenty of grass for him to eat every day. As time went on, there is no doubt in my mind I liked this goat and he was just the right size for me to ride. Even though I was short and young, he too was short and so young that it wasn't difficult for me at all. I just sit down on his back and held on to his horns with my two feet slightly touching the ground and then make annoying noises for him to move or, if not, slap his bottom. This little goat was also my very first time to ever ride an animal. When I rode him, one of my brothers would have to watch me, in case the goat would go wild. I was close to this little creature because he let me ride him. He wasn't scared of me and I wasn't scared of him. We kept the little goat tied to a peg in the vacant lot across the street where we also sometimes kept a cow—whenever my family could afford it—which we would fatten on the grass that grew all across the lot before it was eventually butchered.

Floro Tumulak (L) and Eutropia Tumulak (R), my Grandpa and Grandma Tumulak.

Back to my grandparents and our original ancestral home, Grandpa Tumulak—or *Lolo* Floro or *Lolo Oplong*, as his kids and wife referred to him—was flamboyant, boastful, and full of himself but everyone loved him dearly. He was a World War II veteran. During the war he had been a member of the 71st Division, a Philippine Guerrilla unit, and had fought along side Americans of the 132nd Infantry Regiment in the hills north of Cebu City. He became wealthy after the war because he found a good man, a Doctor Velencia, who gave him a great opportunity to care for a large commercial fish pond that the doctor owned on Mactan Island. The doctor was quite wealthy and owned a lot of land in the Lapu-Lapu and Car-Car areas of Cebu province. My father said the Doctor was very kind to my grandfather. My grandfather was placed in charge of maintaining the pond, raising the fish, and harvesting them for the doctor, who then sold them throughout Cebu. During the harvest season when fish were big enough to sell, the doctor had my grandfather collect a large crop to be sold. Once the doctor had sold as much as he could he would tell Grandfather to go ahead and get all he wanted. Apparently that was how he paid my grandfather for his work. Lolo Floro would then gather up all the fish that was left in the pond and sell them for himself, use some to feed his family, and give still others away to his friends and neighbors. This went on year after year after the war and Lolo was able to build a big house and make many friends. He was looked up to in the community and was well thought of by nearly everyone. Of course, sometimes Lolo would get carried away with his very fortunate circumstances. Sometimes he would "smoke" fifty-peso notes in front of others to impress them. At other times he would take his *barkadas*—close friends—to the beach and buy as many as five *lechon*, roasted pigs, to feed everyone at the beach. Sometimes Grandma, or *Lola Toping* as we called her, would get upset because, according to her, Grandpa would often feed his friends and acquaintances and even strangers while his own family and grandchildren did without. But I don't know why she would complain so much because she had her own vice. During these years she would sit out in the yard and play mahjong with people from all around the neighborhood, and wager on those games, all day long. It was no wonder, then, with Grandma's gambling and Grandpa giving everything away that they became so well-known and well-liked throughout the community. They both had friends and acquaintances from every walk of life—policemen friends and criminal friends; doctor and lawyer friends and out-of-work friends. In fact, for many years—up until I got married and moved away—any of us kids, or anyone for that matter, could get into a trike or taxi anywhere on Mactan Island or in certain portions of the Cebu City area and simply say their destination was "Floro" and the driver would drop them off near our Grandparent's house!

A typical Spanish-influenced Filipino house of the 1950s and 1960s,
quite similar to my Grandpa and Grandma Tumulak's home.

The front of their home was quite close to the street. Closer than my parent's little Nipa hut. On the other side of my grandparents' house was the little house of my Uncle Rudy, my mother's brother. It was not a big house, just big enough for his family, but I always liked that house because of the way Uncle Rudy designed the inside. Because of that, and I guess I was naive at the time, in my childish little opinion, I always thought his family's house was a lot better than mine. As I think back, perhaps he was also jealous of us. He was always full of himself. He and his oldest son were constantly saying something to hurt my feelings. To be honest, I never liked Uncle Rudy very much. He and his son would always make fun of me—about my height, because I was short, or tease me about my flat nose. On the other hand I liked his wife, Aunt Carmen, very much. She had suffered from T.B. for many years and as a result always looked thin and sickly but Aunt Carmen was the nicest of all my aunts that I have ever met. I guess, in a way, she made up for Uncle Rudy in that family. She was too kind, though. I felt sorry for her not only because of her illness but also because her daughter was always taking advantage of her. Uncle Rudy was a carpenter and built many houses. He probably also had more money than my family because he had clients who were always seeking him out to build them a house. But he was always comparing his family to my family and once even told my parents they should just save their money and pull me out of school because none of *his* children wanted to finish their education. In fact, since he made pretty good money, that is probably why his children were always taking advantage of him and Aunt Carmen and never wanted to finish anything. They could always rely on their father and his money. Uncle Oscar, another brother of my mother, also lived on my grandparents' land, behind their big house and Uncle Rudy's. Uncle Oscar, another of my mother's brothers—she had eight brothers and four sisters—was a good guy and my favorite Uncle. I always felt sorry for him, too, because even though he never complained, I think he was sad and disappointed with the location he had been given for his house. The family water-well was close by and all the drainage canals ran near Uncle Oscar's home. Whenever anyone pumped water at the well, the runoff flowed all around his house and the canals usually remained wet or damp throughout the day and evening, leaving a breeding-ground for mosquitoes or *Lamoks*, as we call them in our language. To the left side of Uncle Oscar's was a small *duhat* tree which bore fruit similar to large black grapes that always fell on the ground all along the side of his house as they ripened. In addition, there was also a water storage area set up here which was used for washing clothes or bathing. It was similar to what American's would call a water trough or tub. Because of the constant dampness surrounding this location, and the fact that houses in the Philippines don't have screens over the windows—only wood shutters or wood slats that open and close—Uncle Oscar's house was full of *Lamok* every night.

Regarding the tub—called a *pasong* in our language—there is a big difference between an American tub and a Filipino tub. The Filipino tub is made of concrete and is located outside the house without any shelter over it. It's usually rectangular shape, about four-feet wide and eight-feet long, and often served as the water storage container for the women as they washed clothes. Although nearly everyone in the area had one, anyone in the immediate neighborhood was welcome to use the *pasong* if it wasn't in use. Some people, like my Great-Uncle Tiago, had two tubs because it had many purposes. Not only was it used as a bathtub and a wash tub, but it was used to water the cattle in the neighborhood, too. Many families in the area raised a cow or two and kept them tied to a peg driven into the ground somewhere in some portion of their yard.

A young Tumulak family including my grandparents, my Mama and all my aunts and uncles. Back row, standing L-R: Uncle Totong, Uncle Rudy, my mother Maxima, Aunt Tesse, Aunt Nayda, Aunt Aling, Uncle Oscar, Uncle Dictivo, and Uncle Dario. Front row, seated L-R: Uncle Glen, Aunt Susan, Uncle Nelson, Grandpa Floro, Grandma Eutropia, Uncle Tonyo and Uncle Fernando.

The final structure built on my grandparents property was a little out-house rest room, called a "comfort room" or "C.R." in my country. For sanitary purposes, it was constructed at the back end of my grandparents' property, far away from the main house. The C.R. was surrounded by a variety of fruit trees such as banana trees on the left side and star-apple trees on the right with a whole bunch of banana trees of different sizes behind it because banana trees grow wild in the Philippines in the moist or swampy areas.

As I was growing up, I remember several times when my mama and grandpa got angry with each other. They would argue over something trivial for several days until, finally, they would seem to hate each other. To my young eyes it looked as though the family bond had collapsed and was no longer in their sight. They seemed to act as enemies. Grandma and my papa knew better than to get involved and stayed out of it. After a while, though, papa would have to go out and get other family members to help him pick up our house and move mama and Grandpa away from each other. So, I remember one time we moved to Uncle Tiago's property and rebuilt our little Nipa house there. It was in this place that I was old enough that I started to observe, learn, and know a few things about life. I had just started the First Grade in school when we moved to this location. Our closest neighbor, of course, was Uncle Tiago, the owner of the land, and on the other side was Aunt Puring. Aunt Puring was the sister of Uncle Tiago and also of Grandma Toping so I guess they were actually my *great* aunt and uncle. I remember this site as a really peaceful place. The number of houses and the number of people in this area was much less back then than there is now. This is when I became best friends with Gemma and Karen. They were sisters. Again, in our "family tree" they were actually my Great-Aunts but because of their ages, I simply referred to them as my cousins, even if it wasn't properly correct. Gemma and I were nearly the same age while Karen was two or three years younger. We enjoyed walking to school and playing together every day but then, a short time later, mama and grandpa became friends again and we moved back to live with my grandparents. Although I missed living near Gemma and Karen, this particular time we moved into one of the rooms that Grandpa and Grandma no longer used in the big main house. It was such a huge home. Back at this time when we did this, the big old house was still luxurious. It was built by my Uncle Abraham, a well known carpenter in our town, in the 1950s. When I think back about the house during this period, I have some really fond memories. The house was so big and beautiful then and its design was so well planned. I loved that big old house during this period—before it fell into such disrepair.

After this we moved several more times from our grandparents house to our house and then back again before my parents finally decided to settle down. Our family was growing bigger and they made a final decision to move the little Nipa house to my grandparents' property to its present-day permanent location on the right side of the big old house. Our family's Nipa hut remained here for a number of years before my parents finally could afford to replace it with the more sturdy structure of cinder-block and wood that a portion of which still occupies the site today.

Growing up I remember my mother always seemed to be lecturing me. Mama had always believed that I would grow up to be just another problem to her. She believed that I would eventually do as many teenage Filipino girls—marry an irresponsible or poor Filipino boy, have one baby after another, and then have to come over to her house and beg her to help buy rice for all my children and to help pay for all their clothes, medicine, and other expenses. Mama used to lecture me about that all the time. She would give me sermon after sermon as I was growing up. I tried to ignore her when she did this but it didn't work. Sometimes I thought she was just being mean and hateful with all those lectures. I thought, sometimes, she just didn't love me. And sometimes I felt as though maybe I was not really her child. I didn't understand then like I do now. I didn't know back then anything about what Americans call depression. I didn't know that someone suffering from it might be angry or worried all the time or do or say cruel things because of it. Back then I didn't see or understand all the daily stress and pressures that my mother had in her life by having so many children—and then grandchildren—to care for and feed every day of her life. Mamma was hardworking but kept her house and children and then grandchildren very clean. She was up every morning by 2 a.m. pumping water and washing clothes by hand—her clothes, her family's clothes, and the married daughter, son-in-law, and grand-children's clothes. If her daughters were there they helped but, like their husbands, they were usually off working odd jobs some place trying to make enough money to feed and care for their large families. As a result, all of the little children or grandchildren were either around mama's house or at school. Papa helped pump water, did various chores, and cooked before he went off to his odd-jobs or to do the necessary errands. After washing everything by hand, mama hung the clothes on lines in the yard to dry and cared for the children, later took down the clothes—earlier if it rained—folded the clothes, and put them away. Meanwhile she swept and cleaned the house and outside walkways, fed the little children around the house and the older ones who came home from school for lunch, all the while tending a little store she had, that was attached to the front of our house, throughout the day. Of course, after each meal dishes or pots and pans had to be washed. By evening papa was home and cooking the evening meal with mama. It was the same routine each and every day. Mama had been doing this since she had been a little girl. Out of necessity she was required to quit school after the third grade and help take care of all of her brothers and sisters while grandpa and grandma were busy. From the age of nine mama was washing all of her family's clothes, taking care of her younger brothers and sisters, washing dishes, cooking the meals for her brother and sisters and parents and cleaning house and all the other necessary chores, including sewing and repairing every ones' clothing. It wasn't uncommon in the

Philippines. Because of the constant necessity to work and help make money for such large families, many had to quit school to help their parents make ends meet. It still goes on today in my country. While I was growing up at home, mama insisted that I help with the wash, the kids, and all the other chores. Of course, at the time I thought she was just being mean. I often rebelled, refused, ran off and hid or, sometimes, even covered myself with the dirty laundry and went back to sleep. What would sometimes look like a pile of wash in the corner of the room was sometimes actually covering me up while I was getting some extra sleep! This made mamma furious. She would notice her pile of wash had become larger and would pick through it as she prepared a load to take outside to begin her wash and all of a sudden she would find me sitting there beneath several items and it would always startle and scare her and make her angry that I was hidding and back sleeping again. She would go berserk!

All of us kids had various responsibilities throughout the day. Mine was to help with the wash, cook the rice, and clean and sweep the house. And each day I resisted as long as I could.

Every day is Wash Day in the Philippines and ALL the girls are required to help.

Mama's Store at the front of our house.
Every day she had a business to run, clothes to wash, and a family to feed.

Back then, my Aunt Vergie—actually the daughter of my grandmother's sister and therefore my mother's first cousin—and her family lived in the next house west of my grandparents property and her aunt Marcila—my great-great aunt—lived to the left, or west side, of her. From my grandparents house all the way down to my Aunt Vergie's,—in fact past her place and stretching back to the next block behind—were the homes of all family members. All of the neighbors within two or three blocks of this area as far as you could see were family. This land was all connected and was all occupied by relatives because my dear great-grandparents had owned almost the entire community of Timpolok at one time—and they had so many children. As each of their children grew up and married, they were given a site to build their house and raise a family, as was the custom. The houses back then were further spaced out and less crowded than they are today. When I was a child, my grandparents still owned most of the land all along the opposite side of the street. Still mostly vacant, they used it to plant a variety of crops such as corn, sweet potatoes, bitter melons, cassava, eggplant and many other vegetables. In fact, this whole area was used to grow plants, vegetables and fruit trees that were all shared among the relatives. There was one little house next to this property, however, that was occupied by a couple that were not related to us. These people, who lived in a little Nipa house they had built there, were the caretakers of a large grove of nearby mango trees not owned by my family. To me and the other kids these people seemed very spooky. I didn't see them out very often and it scared or surprised me when they did come around. They seemed to act differently than other people. Many of us thought they were witches especially with their weird look. Mama always said that this couple owned a long *latigo,* or horse whip. My mom often threatened that if I behaved badly or didn't do my chores she would go to the couple and borrow their *latigo.* On the other side or left of their property was a large corn field owned by a farmer named Mahalaleel. For a time, he rented the vacant lots in this area from many of my relatives and planted a lot of corn and a few casava. He actually lived on the other side of town, in the Carajay community, but because his land there was small with no room for his corn-growing business—which was how he made his living—he had asked each of my ralatives who were owners of the surrounding vacant lots to let him pay rent and use the land. Mahalaleel became quite well-known in our community because of his character. He was what you would call in America a stand-up comedian, a jokester, and he would often draw a crowd wherever he went. Even at a young age I was overtaken by him and became one his followers. He would peddle his bicycle from Carajay to our barrio and stop by mama's store for a coca-cola, some rest, some fellowship, and shade before going on to his cornfield. As he talked to the others, I would listen to all of his stories about his experiences and his family as he joked about them. I enjoyed every word he would say. But because he was so energetic and comical—a regular jokster—he was often invited to help with the cooking at many of our neighborhood parties, including funerals, weddings, birthdays and fiestas, and because he was so popular and worked so much farm land all by himself—some people said he was a witch. People in my country are quick to make such judgements about who are witches and who are not. Sometimes if someone is very popular someone else, behind their back, will say they must be a witch and have cast a spell on the others. But if you look dirty and smell like a fish they will also think you are a witch as well as if you're old but strong and in good health and can do a lot of things. Then too, if you're sick and acting weird, especially delirious or waving your arms and hands, that is also considered a sign of witch behavior. So, as you can imagine, nearly any behavior could cause you to be called a witch if people don't know you or if you are from a different area. Many of the older people still hold such superstitions and beliefs to this day. Most of those in Lapu-Lapu are still all kin to one degree or another and have inherited their land down through their families. Generally they are suspicious of any outsiders and do not trust them. In Mahalaleel's case, he was able to overcome most of this because of his personality. He was very charismatic In his later years he become a pastor in a protestant church

When I was a little bitty girl, very young maybe about four or five years old, my neighborhood—Gun-ob, Timpolok—was really quiet. The street that now runs along the front of my parents' house was not yet available for public use. It was simply an unpaved wide path or roadway. Back then we had to walk a few miles to reach or find public transportation in order to reach the destination we wanted to go. When we wanted to go to the market in nearby Lapu-Lapu City we had to walk a few blocks in either direction to get transportation. One direction was as close as the other from our house because we were in the middle of the block. To the right a few blocks was Timpolok street and to the left was Babag. Actually Babag was a main highway so most people in our neighborhood went to that location because a lot of motorcycles—called "trikes" or "motor-trikes" because they are motorcycles with a one-wheeled large roofed sidecar attached that holds several people—come by along that road most often. The closest school to our neighborhood was Babag-1, a public school for elementary and high school students only. Remembering back as a little girl, a long time before, it seems the site was used as a cemetery but somehow suddenly it became a school property. The closest college or university to our neighborhood was the University of San Carlos five or six miles (10 km) away in the big City of Sugbo (Cebu), which is often referred to as the Queen City of the South.

Our home, in Gun-ob, Timpolok, is on the west side of Mactan Island near the Mactan International Airport, the country's second largest. The fish farm where my Grandfather—and later my father—worked as a caretaker was located within the approach to the airport runways. As my papa worked, we kids would often play in the area but, when I was very young, I would always run and hide behind a palm tree whenever the big loud planes would fly over, taking off or landing. They scared me so. I thought it was a big giant bird, the *owak* or hawk-bird, that would come to get me as my mother had so often threatened. After all, at the time I didn't really know what an owak was for sure. Those planes didn't seem to affect or worry all the other kids, though, but they scared me very much.

As I grew older I learned there was actually people inside those airplanes and, although I would still run and hide when I heard them approaching, I would slowly peek out from behind the tree and watch intently as it passed, wondering who might be on that airplane and where they might have been.

As a little girl I was amazed to learn that this giant "bird" actually had people inside.

CHAPTER 2

As School Begins, Trouble Ascends

Today it is unbelievable to me when my mind drifts back to my past—when my thoughts visit my beginnings as a little girl and continue through becoming a full-grown women. The challenges of life back then sometimes just don't seem real. I can't imagine how we survived. Yet, our situation at the time did not seem out of the ordinary. It was no different than that of most of our neighbors or many others that we knew. But now it's amazing to think back about how we ever got enough food or lived in such crowded conditions—so many of us in just a single room. We were a family of eight including my parents. Imagine no privacy, just a simple little house. At night we all slept together side by side—in a position not unlike sardines. And now, today, I am so proud and grateful for ALL of what I have experienced. My past is a treasure to me that helps me appreciate the things I have now. It has provided me a good lesson and has given me unequaled inspirations to become a better person than I ever could without such experiences.

I didn't realize it then, but all the wealth of America could never buy what we had growing up. We had such treasures in our lives for being so poor. I remember at night, as we all laid huddled together ready for sleep, Papa would begin telling us stories. We kids would lay there and listen to our Papa's voice in the darkness as he told us stories all about his life or told us stories about Mama. Other nights he would talk about us kids or tell us stories about history or even scary stories about monsters, witches or vampires. Our most favorite, though, were the stories he told having riddles and paradoxes with questions that we were required to answer and the numerous adventures he told about regarding our Great-Uncle Kayo who fought off demons with his powers of prayer. Papa was such a great story teller and his tales bring back fond memories but I also remember that as we laid in the dark and listened so intently, we would all drift off to sleep one by one, unable to keep our eyes open for very long.

The Avenido family, back row L-R: Helen, Melba, mama Maxima,
papa Claro, Vilma, Front row L-R: Carlito, Richein, Ferdinand.

Thinking back about those early years, I could never understood how Mama always knew what we kids were doing. Especially those times when we were doing something we were not supposed to be doing. I think she must have had a Secret Service workin' for her. Perhaps she bribed my cousins with chocolate or something from her store to tell her everything they knew or saw. I remember climbing way up high into a tree one time. Higher than I was ever supposed to go. Mama was nowhere around. By the time I had climbed down, there she was waiting beneath the tree with a switch in her hand. My feet had barely touched the ground before she was beating me with that stick. One other time I was hiding and eating candy in our store. As I finished and came out into the open, there was Mama standing there with a stick. I need say no more. She was bound and determined to teach all of her kids right from wrong.

Then too, I really hated how mama used to wake all of us up early in the morning to do our chores before we left for school. Sometimes she would abruptly pull the covers back and slap us on the butt, or pinch or bite our ear, or sometimes she would hold a lighted candle over us and let the hot melted wax drip onto our arm, our hand, or onto the soles of our bare feet. Anything to annoy us to the extent that we would get up. Americans today might call something like this abuse but mama had six kids to get up every morning and had no time to keep coming back to wake up those who had rolled over and tried to get some extra rest. Back when she had tried to be nice and gently wake each of us, we all ignored her and simply rolled back over and fell back asleep as soon as she had left the room. Americans who would call Mama's tactics abusive have no idea how lovingly she cared for us or took care of us at other times, especially when we were sick. To this day I miss her care when I am ill. I miss here rubbing vaporizing ointment on me when my chest is congested, Efficascent Oil on my stomach when I'm having cramps, or gently massaging my temples or forehead when I have a headache or even her gently brushing my hair in front of the mirror as she sat and talked with me at bedtime. Sometimes I am able to persuade my husband to rub Vicks or Efficascent Oil on me when I need it but not without hearing complaints. Today he is more willing, knowing how much I miss my mother's gentle touch but, of course, it will never be the same and he realizes that.

When I was a child, a family of eight required at least 3,612 peso per month, or P43,344 per year. That translates to about 120 U.S. dollars a month or just over $1,444/year. In comparison to today, to cover the basic necessities of life, a family of this size now needs at least 13,600 pesos per month, or the equivalent of over $340US. As I was growing up we lived on a diet of fish—we especially enjoyed fresh milk-fish, shrimp, tilapia, blue crab, and other shellfish—and rice, occasionally supplemented by additional meat such as chicken or pork, and fresh vegetables. We also had an abundance of fresh fruit available all around our house.

Although the neighborhood school I attended, Babag 1, was a public school, we were still required to wear a prescribed uniform similar to those of the private Catholic schools. In our school boys wore a white shirt with navy pants and white socks while the girls were required to wear a white blouse with a maroon gingham dress and white socks. Our family being poor, of course, required that I wear the hand-me-downs from my sister Vilma. Even at that, we could only afford one uniform per child so when we were young Mama would wash our uniforms and hang them up to dry by morning. As we became older, each of us were required to wash our own school uniform and make certain it was hung up and dry by school-time the following day. Sometimes I would get it done and sometimes I would forget and had to fake it the next day. Anyway, by the time Vilma had outgrown each dress and it got to me, its color was usually dull or faded and it had been repaired a number of times. It was another source of my embarrassment at school as I was growing up.

Babag 1 Elementary School where I attended. This photograph,
taken the day before summer vacation was to began, shows these children
being given freedom from the dress-code during the last day of school.

It is true that we have so much poorness in the Philippines but we have so much richness too. Cebu and Mactan Island are literally paradises for fruit lovers. There is nearly a never-ending variety. Banana trees grow wild. There is also fresh pineapple and papayas, juicy jumbo yellow mangos—said to be the best in the world—*attis* or custard apples, *balimbing* or star fruit, chico, and huge delicious jack fruits. Simply walking down the street in the Philippines is like walking down the fruit and produce section of your local grocery store in America, except its fresher, and if the fruit tree isn't on a vacant lot—simply free for the taking—we often ask or buy fruit from the resident of the yards where the trees are growing as we pass by. Sea foods are abundant too. There are shellfishes of every kind just for the taking too. Prawns, or jumbo shrimp, as long as the palm of your hand and two fingers wide, are abundant. And Blue crabs and King crab, octopus and squid and fish of every type are in the waters surrounding us. Each morning before we left for school, Papa would fix us a good breakfast of fish and rice.

Often times he rose long before first light and went to the fish pond or, in later years, to the fish market, to get something fresh to fix his children to eat. I guess you could say being poor in the Philippines has its advantages. When we eat, we eat fresh fruit, fresh vegetables, and fresh seafood. It is not like in America where you buy a week's worth of food and store it away or plan your weekly menu. In the Philippines you don't plan a day or two ahead. Each day is consumed with what you're gonna fix for breakfast, what you're gonna have for lunch, and what can you afford to get for dinner. So your food is always fresh because you go out and get it shortly before each meal.[1] At lunch time all the children return to their homes for their noon-time meal, a short rest, and then return for the remainder of school classes. Again, Papa or Mama have run out and gotten something to fix for lunch to go along with the rice—a "partner" for the rice—and maybe even the grandparents and an Aunt or Uncle or two have stopped by the house waiting to eat with the children at the noon meal.

When I was in the first grade, I recall that I would always arrive an hour or two early before the class began in order to clean our class room. My teacher, Mrs. Ulanda Manos, would reward any of us kids when we came in early to help make our classroom neat and clean. I always got the reward because I came in before anyone else and tried so hard to sweep and straighten up our room. That first year of school I always did my best to try and please my teacher. I guess I was always trying to get the praise from her that I wanted to hear from my mama.

Mrs. Manos was also our neighbor and sometimes she would ask me and my neighborhood friends to take things over to her house on our way home. Nearly every day the fish or vegetable vendors would come by the school at the end of the class and she would often choose a few good, fresh items and have us children take them to her house while she finished up her work. We would take them by and give them to her maid and pass along any instructions that Mrs. Manos might have told us. When Mrs. Manos went out on leave because she was having a baby, she was replaced by Mrs. Sandoval, Mrs. Sandoval was very strict. I remember that one day one of our classmates, Renanti, got punished by her for being so rude while she was trying to explain some lesson to the class. She brought Renanti to the front of the group and pulled his shorts down in front of us. Of course he, like the rest of us, his family was poor and he wasn't wearing any underwear and we all laughed. Before this day, Renanti had always been our class clown. He was always making faces and making some kind of remark or comments to make the class laugh but he was so embarrassed by this that he behaved well after that. I guess you could say Mrs. Sandoval gave him his own private lesson to behave in front of the class—sort of his own tutoring session.

My fondest first grade memory was reading. I loved reading *Henny Penny*. My biggest problem was my handwriting. I had a lot of trouble with my penmanship. As my first grade year came to a close, we had our First Grade Presentation—in which I eagerly participated. Our choreographers for this event was my uncle Fernando and Saida Manos, the daughter of our teacher. They chose "Pop-Pop Girl" as the dance number and since I was known in the neighborhood for being a good dancer because I could easily follow any steps I was shown as if I was born with the talent, they made me the lead. Everyone, it seemed, enjoyed watching. Even at six years old I could really shake my hips and wiggle my butt to the music.

My Second Grade year was highlighted by the memorization of the poem "All Things Bright and Beautiful." I became very good at reciting this because I loved the poem and even today it is still dear to my heart. I still enjoy reciting it. My second grade teacher was Mrs. Flanco, who I liked very much because she is very soft spoken.

My Third Grade teacher was Mrs. Ulanda Dungog. She was very strict and probably the most scariest teacher in our elementary school at the time. Mrs. Dungog called me the most talkative person in her class and she didn't mean it as a complement. Once in a while she would make the boys and girls set side by side to avoid talking. At that age girls don't usually like to talk with boys so she would achieve her goal of having a peaceful class when she did that. One time I asked her permission to go out and relieve myself. I don't know why, but I was rather crass about it. Perhaps I was rebellious with Mrs. Dungog because I associated her behavior or strictness with my mother's. I really don't know why I behaved the way I did in her class. But I remember that when I raised my hand to be excused she seemed to ignore me so I yelled at her to get her attention. She was talking to some visitor or perhaps a parent and I was getting desperate so I called out in a the loud voice, "Ma'am! I must go poop!" She was totally embarrassed. She walked over and grabbed me and put her finger up close to my face and shook it, saying she didn't like my attitude, I was *bastos*—indecent, course or gross—and had no respect. I saw a look in her eyes that I will never forget. After that incident I became more fearful of her and I did my best never to make her mad at me again. In looking back, I must say she was probably one of the best and smartest teachers in the school.

When I was going on ten years old and anticipating on beginning the fourth grade, I found out that I had to quit school. The cost of sending Vilma to school was becoming an overwhelming burden to my parents and they said they just could not afford to send me to school any more. Helen had already quit school after graduating from grade school and was working in a little shell-craft factory and my two older brothers had already quit and were both working at the fish pond with Papa. The cost of Vilma's tuition fees, notebooks and school projects, on top of our family's food and clothing costs and other bills had just become too much I was told.

My parents sat down with me and my brothers and tried to explain why we would all have to stop going to school. I screamed out in agony. I didn't like their decision and didn't want to believe them but they tried to explain they didn't have a choice. They apologized to each of us and, I think, were truly sorry, but they said they had to do this. They explained we wouldn't be able to start back to school or me and my brothers might have to postpone school for a while because we all had a long way to go. Vilma, our hope for the future, would continue, they told us. They were hoping our family situation would not get worse, they said, or none of the rest of us would ever be able to continue our studies.

I was devastated. I didn't like what was happening to me. I didn't like what was happening to my life. I didn't like what was happening to my family. Life, it seemed, just was not fair.

It hurts so much to think back about this and it is probably one of the most hurtful moments of my childhood experience. It caused me so much shame and embarrassment at the time, especially with my classmates. For a whole two year period I was living with fear. Fear of being seen by any of the kids or past classmates from my school. When I did see them I would run and hide. I just couldn't stand to face them. I had so much *hiya*—deep pride and shame—and I couldn't face the reality of not going to school like everyone else. I felt great pity for myself thinking I would grow old and always be illiterate. I wanted to learn so badly. I wanted knowledge and to be smart. I remember thinking that I did not want this happening to me. It was a nightmare. This was the first time I can remember ever being jealous—or envious—of others. No one knows that except me. I was jealous of the other kids that they could continue in school while I had to quit. I thought it was very unfair. Grandpa Floro offered to help me by paying for my schooling but my mom, out of pride herself, refused. She told me that if she allowed Grandpa to help, all the other relatives would talk, the school might demand more than he could afford and she couldn't take that chance, and she needed a house helper anyway and I was the "Number 1" person for that on her list.[2] "Besides," she told me, "you will never make me proud in school like Vilma, who always gets first honors." And, it was true. Vilma was very smart in school. She always got high grades. She was well-liked by all of her teachers—who always compared all the other Avenido children to her as they came up through school—and it was Vilma with whom our family's future would lie. Whether our family ever had enough money for food, medicine, and housing, would always depend on the success of Vilma. That day Mama really made it clear that she had put all of her eggs in one basket. All of her hopes and dreams for the future depended on Vilma!

After I had quit school I helped Mama with the wash and housekeeping each day. At the same time, at the ages of 10 and 11, my Grandmother assigned me the job at her house next door similar to being a Pit-Boss of a casino. Grandmother owned a complete set of tiles for Mahjong games and several decks of cards. Although many of our neighbors and acquaintances enjoyed gambling with these, few owned their own at the time. Every day several games were in operation throughout the house—or in the yard when the weather was good—and it was my job to go around and collect the "rent" or fee for the use of her cards and Mahjong tiles at the end of each game. The winners were also required to pay "the house"—my grandmother—a percentage of their winnings which I also collected. It was during this time that my mathematic abilities greatly improved and I became much quicker and more proficient at calculating than I had ever been in school. When mama found out what I was doing, she became quite angry at Grandmother for exposing me to such bad influences. However, even against her wishes, my job with my grandmother continued for quite some time afterwards because it provided me with spending money.

It was also in 1987, when I was 10, that I learned another great lesson about life. On June 1 of that year my Aunt Aling married her longtime sweetheart Juan. It was a big event in my family. Aunt Aling was very smart—a college graduate—but she was very plain looking and only had one tooth at the time. Grandpa Lo-Lo always referred to her—his own daughter—as a "guitar face." Many in the family didn't believe she would ever marry until she met Juan. He was a nice man and somewhat handsome but, he couldn't see very well. Sunlight hurt his eyes. During the daytime he would walk around with his eyes nearly squeezed shut and had trouble seeing but in the evening, or after dark, he could see fine. So, while some people thought he was somewhat strange, many in our family thought he was a witch. I think he might have realized this, too, because he would often go out of his way to be nice to everyone and often brought gifts to our family. But he also apparently never brushed his teeth back then which caused many in our family to be reluctant to get too close to him or to accept any food from him. Richein and I, on the other hand, loved Juan—not because of his looks but because he always brought us a present nearly every morning when he came to visit Aunt Aling. The present was usually a little square of sweet rice that was wrapped up in a banana leaf, that we call *bud-bud* or *suman* in tagalog. While Mama and the others would say "Don't eat that!" Richein and I would gladly eat it and people would then say, "Yeah, yeah, go ahead and eat it. I bet he is casting a spell on you when you eat that."

Uncle Juan was—and still is—a very good man. I always felt sorry for him and Aunt Aling because so many others always seemed to make fun of them back then. People can be so cruel sometimes. Their marriage that year had a profound influence on my life forever after. I came to realize, and still truly believe, that everything and everyone fits a purpose that God has created. Uncle Juan and Aunt Aling seemed so different from many of the others, they were a perfect match for each other. No matter why we are the way we are, we all have someone who is just right for us. When you think about it in the same way, even in a rocky, barren terrain, what someone might consider weeds growing along a steep bank eventually sprout wild flowers that not only beautify the site but later produce an abundance of seeds to feed the birds and to reproduce the wild flowers the following year. Everything and everyone has a reason to be here the way they are. Whether it is immediately apparent to everyone or not, God has a purpose for everything and every body. This gave me hope for myself too. So often people in my family had made fun of me for being short or having a flat nose.

Ever since those days of the1980s, Uncle Juan has continued to operate a successful coconut vinegar business. He has always been a hard worker and his product has always been considered the best quality and very popular in the Cebu region. Even Mama admits his product is the best around. He climbs the trees, himself, to collect only the best coconuts to use and produce the best possible vinegar. At nearly 67 years old, he still does. That is how he originally met Grandpa Lo-Lo and Auntie Aling. In his business, Juan went around the various neighborhoods and paid landowners for permission to climb their coconut trees and to gather the best *lubi*.[3]

After two whole years, I was able to go back to school. It was the 1988-89 school year and I was 11 years old, going on 12. Little Richein was just beginning the First Grade.[4] I was unhappy about being two years older than most of my classmates but I had the choice of being ashamed of my age for beginning the fourth grade or staying illiterate and working hard at home. I hated the housework so much and I wanted knowledge so badly, so I chose to go back. At first my classmates were a little hard on me because of my age but I was able to put them in their place. They soon learned that I could do a lot of stuff that they didn't know how to do and that I knew a variety of ways and many different games in order to have fun. To some I became a hero because I tried to protect them from the bullying kids. Even though I was small for my age, in this grade I felt superior. I tried to be protective of all my classmates and to help them. Still, I did have a lot of fighting going on, especially with the boys who were always trying to make the girls cry. These particular students were always making up stories such as who had a crush on who or who was liking who among our classmates. And a few of the girls were having their first menstruation and if something happened and the boys found out about it, they would make fun of them or when some of the girls began developing breasts, these boys always had crude comments about it. All of these things are traumatic to girls this age and although I didn't always understand it myself, I always felt protective of them and tried to help. I, too, had a crush on boys in this class and in some of the other classrooms by this time but I had to keep it to myself, knowing that if anyone was to ever find out they would make fun of me too. So I went through the entire school year without revealing those crushes to anyone. I knew I would loose my strength in the class if anyone found out about those crushes and there would be no one left to protect my friends. I remember this school year as having the power of the boys and I didn't want to loose that. But I also remember it as the year when I first realized I had feelings for boys. I enjoyed this class-year very much and I enjoyed getting back into school.

The year was not, however, without its problems. Along with my embarrassment about my age and being the oldest in the class, another incident occurred which nearly made me quit school forever. At the time, I didn't think I could ever live through it.

I had a constant "thirst" for knowledge. One day at school they handed out a pamphlet describing all about a number of books we could buy along with an order blank. I read through the little pamphlet and found several books that greatly interested me. I ordered three and wanted them very badly. The first was a Karate Dictionary. I liked the dictionary because I thought it was cool and I could use it to defend myself more efficiently from my enemies. I loved the action-movie-star Jackie Chan and wanted to have moves like him. The second book I ordered was an English Dictionary because I wanted to learn to speak and write English fluently. And the third was a Math Dictionary because it was my hardest subject and I wanted to learn to master it. I loved what I had learned so far about what could be done in math, especially the multiplication computations. I was very happy and proud of myself that day as I walked home from school with my order receipt. I looked at it and read it over and over on my way home, excited and happy, anticipating the arrival of these wonderful books in just a few weeks. I couldn't wait! And I knew Mama would be so proud of my renewed interest in learning.

When I got home, I proudly showed Mama the receipt for the books and enthusiastically began telling her all about them. I was immediately interrupted by her yelling. As an American might say, she hit the roof! She was mad! She told me I had no right to order any books without her permission; that we couldn't afford them and she had no idea how we were gonna pay for them. She wanted me to go cancel the order. I told her "Mama, they're already ordered. Please, I'll be embarrassed." I remember her asking me if I thought I was rich and then telling me I was so full of baloney. I was shocked. I didn't know what to do. I didn't know what to say. I just couldn't believe she wasn't happy that I wanted to learn. I ran up stairs, sat down, and sobbed and cried throughout the night. Everything seemed so unfair. I just knew that I couldn't go back to school and face the other students and have them all know I couldn't afford those books. And I couldn't go back and face the teacher, Mrs. Bensi, a distant relative of my grandfather, or the other school officials after ordering books that wouldn't be paid for. The teacher or the school would surely have to pay for them or at least have to pay to have them sent back, I worried. Now, it seemed, I couldn't go back to school again.[5]

The next day I *didn't* go to school. I was too embarrassed. Mama didn't seem to care. She told me that if I had shame, I had to help with the housework to "earn my bread." I continued to stay home from school day after day, doing the housework and hanging out with Grandpa, taking care of him and making money. Grandpa always gave me a peso to bring him water, lead him to the toilet, or to do various chores for him. One day, after several weeks, Mrs. Bensi sent some of my classmates to my house to find out what had happened to me and to tell me it was OK to come back to school. It had been nearly a month. I still had my school assignment book and I was going to give it to them to turn in for me when one of them said, "Melba, Mrs. Bensi said that if you come back to school and can pass a test, you can still continue." They also revealed that she had also told them that I was a very good student and had made good grades and it would be a big waste not to continue. Having heard that, and having my pride somewhat returned, I went with them to school that day and talked with Mrs. Bensi and worked everything out. I never did learn what had happened to those books I had ordered nor was the subject ever brought up again after that.

In the fifth grade it seems my school life, such as it was, returned to normal. My teacher then, Mr. Hilig, caught me sleeping, with my head laying on my desk, and as he came down the isle during his lecture he flicked the end of my nose with his pointer stick and said, "Did you go overtime at the disco last night?"

Again, I was totally embarrassed. He had no idea of how cruel his remark was to me. All I can say in my defense, today, is that I had been up all night helping the family with Mama who had been suffering from high blood pressure at the time and had a stroke the night before. She was extremely ill at the time. We couldn't afford to get her medical attention or to summon a doctor, so we all helped her the best we could throughout the days and nights before and after this incident at school until she was able to regain her health. Many days after this it was difficult for me to keep my eyes open and to listen to his boring lectures but after this extreme embarrassment it became very important to me not to let my eyes fall shut again in his class.

I remember another traumatic experience I had at about this time. Mother always thought I was a good singer and always encouraged me to perform in front of others. Dancing or singing was always my talent for the "Miss Universe" games we played in the neighborhood. I preferred dancing and had always danced in a number of school pageants but I liked to sing too. In fact, I remember that my Mother always seemed so happy when she was watching me sing. Thinking back, I can still see the smile on her face as she watched. I guess she regarded Vilma as her smart girl and she regarded me as her singer or entertainer.

Melba, age 6, in one of her dancing performances.

When I was thirteen and in the sixth grade, Mama arranged for me to sing in our barrio's April Youth Festival pageant. At her urging and because of my passion for dancing, I had volunteered to dance in our town's fiesta along with my younger brother and a childhood friend. But Mama had also entered me in an amateur singing contest. First prize was one-thousand Peso. Singing in front of our own family or in front of others in our "Miss Universe" games was one thing but officially performing in front of an large audience of people I did not know—and for money—was quite another! I was nervous just thinking about it but I practiced my song, "One Week of Love" nearly every morning and every evening for a week. Mama went out and purchased a Minus-One tape of the song for me to practice. A Minus-One tape is a recording of the song that allows the listener to eliminate or turn down the vocal portion, leaving only the music portion to practice to. They are, of course, much more expensive than a simple tape of the song. Finally, after a lot of practice and instruction by Mama, the evening of the competition arrived. As my family and many friends, neighbors and relatives sat out in the audience in anticipation, I remember hearing the Master of Ceremonies announce "Contestant Number 5," who was me. Mama and the rest of the family sat up on the edge of their seats to see what I would do. Back when I was five I had walked out onto the stage, forgot the words to the song and ran off and hid and Mama finally had to go find me. I'm sure some of my uncles and their families sitting out in the audience were hoping I would do that again. They all had talked about that incident and had laughed about it for years. This time Mama knew I was scared and nervous. Back stage, carrying her stick, she had told me 'don't you ever waste the money that I spend on you' and she used the stick for emphasis but she also gave me a little shot of Tanduay Rum to relax me while a number of my Aunts and Uncles had given me advise. They told me just to imagine that all of those faces in the audience were nothing but coconuts. They had all come to the house over the past few days and had listened to me practice, telling me I was good, and my Aunt Oyang came over to visit each day had massaged my back telling me she "had the power of God" in her fingers and it would help me with my performance. On each visit she would ask me to sing my song for her and then after I finished she would tell me how much she loved my voice. She worked so hard to help build up my confidence that week. I barely remember walking out onto the stage. I was so timid and shy, but I sang my song and although I didn't win, I succeeded in completing my performance. Afterwards I was embarrassed because I had missed up some of the lyrics. Mama was disappointed too. She got no prize money for her investment but she gave me plenty of housework to do the following morning. She vowed never to waste her money on me again.

Another event in the sixth grade greatly influenced my future and taught me another valuable lesson about the importance of honesty and integrity. One of the smartest girls in our class, Lenny-Lin Pahugot, had changed the grade on her report card before taking it home to her parents to sign. Our teacher, Mrs. Solano, noticed it immediately when it was brought back to be turned in days later.

Perhaps Lenny-Lin was under pressure to get good grades or maybe she just wanted to be on the honor role. Whatever her reasoning, the shame and embarrassment Lenny-Lin suffered as a result, was far worse than what she would have ever suffered at her home or in the community had she just taken the responsibility for her lower grade and left it alone. At first, school authorities were not going to allow her to graduate from elementary school but then decided to give her the diploma but not to allow her to attend the ceremony. It was a great embarrassment to her and to her family. I felt deeply sorry for her but realized that she had caused her own pain.

The year 1991 marked the end of the Sixth grade and graduation from Elementary School for me. I was 14 years old and very proud and happy that I had succeeded in over-coming a number of obstacles, both real and imagined.

In the Philippines we go from elementary school graduation of the sixth grade directly into high school. Like many European countries, we do not have a junior high or middle school curriculum as there is in the United States. In the Philippines, our primary and secondary education consists of a total of ten years instead of twelve to prepare us for our lives or for entry into a college or university.

My graduation from elementary school was a personal triumph.

CHAPTER 3

Daily Life in the Philippines

I didn't even own the white dress that I needed for my grade school graduation. It had to be borrowed. At Mama's urging, I borrowed it from our neighbor who had a girl who had graduated two years before. I also had to have a white dress for confirmation at church and had to borrow that dress from my cousin. I always had to be nice to Helen and Vilma, too, so I could borrow some of their dresses for special occasions at school or for church every Sunday. In fact, I didn't have any nice shoes for church either. Helen would sometimes get mad at me because I would use some of her really nice shoes for church. I would have to wad up newspaper to put in the toes to make them fit. My having to borrow usually made her mad because she would never refuse my need but whenever she needed me to do things for her, I was usually always unavailable, watching TV or playing somewhere.

For everyday use, all of us kids wore sandals (chinelas) or what Americans call "flip-flops." Flip flops, however, don't last very long. The way they are made, they always have some part that will quickly become dysfunctional or go kaput after a short time; at least the ones we could afford to buy. When they did separate or some part would break, unlike Americans who would simply throw them away and buy replacements, we Filipino kids grew up learning how to repair them quickly so they could be worn again. One method we used was to use a candle to melt the end of the thong which usually broke or separated from the bottom of the shoe. The heated end could then be flattened out after being reinserted in the sole to help hold it in place. Sometimes, though, when we ran out of luck and the sandal couldn't be fixed, we would go out and find another for the same foot that had been lost or discarded by someone else and use it. When we were little kids, it made no difference if they were different colors as long as we had feet protection during play. We tried all kinds of tricks to make the sandals last but there were times we just had to let it go because it was completely wore out. Even in that case we would get one last use of it by throwing it in the fire to help cook our food. Leather shoes were never used by us kids for play or for everyday use. In fact, it wasn't unusual for some Filipino families not to have them at all but, in this respect at least, our family was luckier than most.

Helen and Vilma had one or two pairs of leather shoes that they kept for special occasions. Our Aunt Tesse and cousin Joy would bring leather shoes for our family every so often. They were ones that our cousins had outgrown. We were always so happy to see Joy and Aunt Tesse come by to visit because the shoes they brought might have been used, with the heels worn down, but they were new and something special to each one of us.

Mama always worked hard to care for her family. She made sure our clothes—what little each of us had—were clean and that our white clothes were as white as they could be. She always kept them washed and repaired and even replaced the elastic in our underwear when it became necessary. She made certain our house was always clean too, whether she cleaned it or made us kids do it, and she always cooked us good meals, often times with the help of Papa, but always freshly prepared and never heated up frozen meals such as is often served up in America. I can remember a lot of times that Mama went 24-hours without sleep because she had to go to the farmers' market to get a good deal on fresh vegetables or fruit. Often times she would head out to the market—along with Papa—at three or four a.m. because by seven the best fruit and vegetables were gone. And other days she always woke up with the crow of the rooster to begin her household chores. In nearly every facet of our lives, it seems, Mama tried very hard to be a good example and to raise all of her children properly. It is no wonder, then, that she developed high blood pressure over the years. We always referred to it as Mama's "high blood" when she would get angry at our failure to behave to her expectations. There were times we were apparently quite frustrating to her although she was doing her best to provide us a good example.

When we were young, I remember her singing lullabies to us at bedtime to help us fall asleep. As we grew older, she would gather us girls together every night to pray before bedtime. We would gather and kneel down around our patron saint, Santo Nino, light candles, and pray and do the Rosary. Sometimes we would hear a crackling noise and smell burning hair as Vilma would fall asleep and lean too far into the candle. Sometimes Vilma would just knock a candle over as she fell asleep and collapsed into the alter. In either case, Mama was usually too busy yelling and putting out the fire than to discipline Vilma. Helen or I would sometimes fall asleep as we were kneeling there praying before the Santo Nino. When that happened, we would often be startled awake by a slap up side our head by Mama. 'Course we would start praying right where we had left off. Vilma sometimes felt Mama's displeasure when she started laughing after one of us made a mistake while reciting the Rosary. 'Course when Vilma started laughing, Helen and I would start laughing, and before we knew it, Mama would slap each of us up side our head. I have since been told by my husband that if an American had ever seen any of this, they probably would have thought it was something out of a "Three Stooges" movie.

Looking back, we were lucky our house never burned down. Vilma was always starting fires, it seems. She was smart in school because she studied hard. Having no electricity in our house until later years, at night we used oil lamps. In fact, after using these lamps each evening, we would often wake up in the morning and have black around the openings of our noses from the soot in the air and black would come out when we blew our noses. Each evening Vilma would sit at the kitchen table or in the bedroom doing her homework. Again, she would sometimes fell asleep and occasionally knock over the oil lamp, breaking its glass globe and spreading burning oil all across our table or floor. One night our curtains caught fire before we could get it put out. On several other occasions she fell asleep while studying by candlelight and the candle melted down and started a fire before she woke up and put it out.

But Vilma also made many sacrifices for us kids as we were growing up. Whenever Mama went to visit or to help Papa during the daytime, we kids played in an area where Papa built and kept the canoes he used on the fish ponds. Vilma watched over and took care of us during these times. Helen was usually off somewhere working to help out our family. So Vilma was usually our babysitter and was responsible for us. I have many fond memories of Vilma carrying Richein and me on her back through the water to avoid the leeches. Rechien and I hated leeches. They sent us into a screaming rampage to see them stuck to us. There was a backwater lagoon that always formed in a low-lying area on the way to the fish ponds during high tide or during the rainy season that was always infested with leeches. Papa had put down large stones in this area so he could cross easily without touching the water but they were too far apart for us kids. Like Papa and Mama, Vilma was big enough to walk from stone to stone so whenever we had to cross this lagoon she would help me and Richein climb up onto her back and hang on tightly around her neck. Poor Vilma would then slowly trudge across the rocks toward dry land, trying to keep her balance and barely able to breathe because of the extra weight and because we were hanging on so tightly. Vilma made many such sacrifices for us like this with never a complaint.

People in the Philippines often rely on the roosters in the neighborhood as their alarm clock. We kids, could easily ignore them. We were use to their early-morning crowing and simply rolled over and went back to sleep. But, in our house Mama was the early bird and, I'm almost sure, she woke the roosters. No doubt her voice woke the neighbors. She could be louder than the roosters, the passing motorcycles, and the neighborhood bread vendors combined. Some people think that life in the Philippines is slow and easy-going but I beg to differ. Every morning Mama would be up before the roosters, immediately waking us kids for chores, and begin to do all of her jobs. According to her, waiting to get up after the sun came out would make you lazy. She had no machines and few appliances and did everything manually—the wash, the mending, the gardening. Each day she had a lot of work to do and insisted we children take care of the overflow. Papa would be up soon after Mama, carrying the water into the house and starting the breakfasts as we kids wandered around the home or out into the yard, nearly delirious in the pre-dawn darkness, trying to wake up and get oriented enough to begin our daily chores.

Once our chores were done and Papa fed us breakfast, we all went off to school. Each of us kids all walked to our school with our own group of friends. These might include some of our classmates who had walked over to our house from theirs to meet up with us, some of our neighbors, and sometimes some of our cousins. My little brother Richein started his schooling back when I had started grade 4 so, per Mama's command, it was my responsibility to walk with him to school each day in order to watch out for him and to protect him. I took him along as I walked with my friends and cousins.

In the Philippines, school begins with a flag ceremony at 7:00 a.m. with classes starting shortly afterward. By 9:00 a.m. we get a thirty-minute recess and are allowed to play outside or to buy a snack if we are hungry. Those who live close to the school are allowed to go home to get a snack. Such snacks might consist of a short stick of sugar cane for about 50-centavos, a small bagful of about a dozen guava with salt or a strip of pineapple on a stick for about the same price, or a fried banana for about 1- to 2-pesos—depending on its size. Drinks would consist of *buko*—or coconut milk,—a Coca-Cola or a Royal True Orange. We go home for lunch at 11:00 with a two-hour break and then back to school at 1:00 for more classes until 4:00. Then we begin our assigned school chores until 5:00 p.m. before going home. Such chores include sweeping and mopping the school room floors, watering plants, cleaning the black boards and going outside to pound the erasers clean, taking out the trash and realigning the desks. Basically we do all of the custodial duties because public schools in the Philippines do not have or hire anyone for the job as is customary in the U.S.A. Once complete, Richein and I, along with our cousins, friends, and neighbors, would all walk home together as we had done at lunchtime.

Sometimes on the way to school one of us had to stop and purchase a pencil or paper. In the Philippines we use our pencils until they are little stubby implements and they are often lost or misplaced when they get that small. I've learned that in America, many stores have displays of school classroom supply lists and needs that the students are required to have on the first day of school each fall. I find that quite amazing. In my county we are lucky to have any school supplies at all let alone be told by our teachers or our other school authorities that we must acquire and bring additional supplies for our school. Each year Mama would buy us each a spiral-ring notebook, a pencil, and maybe an additional package

A typical morning on our way to school. L-R: Me, Ferdinand, Helen and Richein.

of notebook paper containing thirty or so leaves or sheets. As school progressed it sometimes became necessary to stop on our way to school at one of the little corner neighborhood stores to buy another sheet or two of paper. It would cost 25-centavos for maybe ten sheets of paper or sometimes you would tell the store keeper you wanted a peso's worth of notebook paper and they would hand you a few sheets. Back in grade school Mama provided us each with a little pack of Crayons at the beginning of school. We were very careful with these because after a while if we needed a Crayon we would have to wait and hope one of the better-off students would give us the stub of one their Crayons or we would be lucky enough to find a stub or two on the way home or on the way to the school that would be big enough for us keep and use. Then, too, each student in the class was assigned throughout the school year to sweep the floor at the end of the school day. Whenever it was my turn, I would sometimes find a pencil or crayon while I was sweeping. Sometimes I would try and return it to my classmate if it had been near their desk and I thought it was theirs. But if I was unable to determine whose it was, and I liked the color, I would keep it to use in my art projects. Mama would always try to give each of us kids a few centavos each morning so that we could buy a little snack at school. Off and on in Mama's struggle with the store, sometimes she barely had enough money to provide each of us snack money and if any of us also needed paper or a pencil, we sometimes had to make a decision if we would use what little we had for supplies or a snack. I always used mine for the school supplies if I needed them. I preferred to be embarrassed about not getting a snack with my classmates than to not have the necessary sheet or two of paper or to suffer the shame of asking one of them to borrow a sheet. At snack time I would just feign not being hungry that day. To me it was better to have no snack than to have no pad of paper.

At lunch time we all walked home to eat the meal that Mama had prepared. Afterwards, I had to help pump the water to clean the lunchtime dishes. We all completed other chores at home during this time and then we rested a while before we walked back to school to finish out the day. As our last class came to an end, Richein would be waiting for me outside my classroom and we would then walk home with our friends, change out of our school uniform and then proceed to do our assigned after-school duties. My assignment was to pump water for Mama's clothes washing—which she continued off and on throughout each day because of the large amount of wash she always had to do for the eight of us—and to help prepare the evening meal. Such preparations might include cleaning vegetables, preparing the fresh spices, and preparing the kettles and pans for ready use We often had a snack when we first got home. By evening Mama and Papa were busy preparing our evening meal, after which we would become involved in some activity or watch TV as long as we kids had worked together and had done a good job of cleaning the table and dishes. There were times that we tried to trick mom in order to expedite the cleaning so that we could watch a particular TV show. Sometimes it worked and sometimes it didn't. The only times we succeeded was when she was tired, otherwise she would inspect our work and find something not right. The trick was to be able to judge correctly when she was too tired to check.

In a poor third-world country like the Philippines, dancing and singing is our greatest form of recreation and entertainment. It is something we can all do that doesn't cost us anything. We can constantly develop our singing and dancing and use it for our amusement without spending any money on it. Of course, money can be spent if desired and available. Karaoke is very popular in the Philippines—in all of Asia, actually. We save our money and often put our money together in order to buy the necessary equipment, speakers, and microphones. Sometimes several families will put their money together to buy these necessities. Families gather around the TV and VCR, CD player or Karaoke machine on many evenings to sing and dance for fun, competition and laughs. On weekends or non-school nights we pass the microphone around among us until late into the evening sometimes. Family, friends, neighbors, aunts, uncles and cousins often all come over to participate. Nobody is left out. Kids barely old enough to sing and walk, adults so old they're unable to walk, and every age in between, take part in a night of karaoke.

Having a small house with so many kids, our parents seldom had much time alone together. At times, Mama would go to the fish pond and stay the night with Papa. He had a small house there made of coconut-leaf matting, among the fish ponds for his use. When Mama did go there for these visits, she would leave Vilma in charge of the family store and in charge of us younger kids because she trusted her. But Mama never knew that after she was gone Vilma would give all of us kids all kinds of snacks from the store to keep us quiet and to leave her alone while she, herself, would often go in and enjoy a lot of the different kinds of snacks. As far as we know, Mama never noticed any of this upon her return the next morning but I'm sure it led to the depletion of our store's profits and the eventual bankruptcies that always followed.

After my sister Helen had quit school she went on to work in the little neighborhood factory making seashell jewelry for a number of years. She then got a job making rattan furniture where she met Loreto. After some time, they married and she and her husband lived in a little Nipa attachment to my Aunt Delia's apartment until they had saved enough money to build their own Nipa house several meters behind my parents' home. Loreto, went on to train as a welder and later obtained a good welding job and they lived quite comfortably and eventually had four children.

Vilma was married on July 27, 1988, when I was 11 years old. Again, Richein and I had always liked her fiancé, Reynaldo, because he had always brought us a gift of food, a little snack, each time he came to visit her. But Mama was mad and upset over this marriage. She had formed many plans in her head for Vilma. Many of my teachers, too, thought it was a shame when they asked me during roll call on opening day of classes if I was any relation to Vilma Avenido. When I answered "yes, she's my sister," they would begin telling me how smart she was and how she was such an excellent student and how they expected me to be just like her. Invariably they would then ask what she was doing, expecting to use her success in school as an example to all my classmates. "She got married and had a baby," I would answer and watch the disappointment on the teacher's face. One even cried at the news.

As we were growing up, I began to notice and always wondered why Mama had never attended any of our parent-teacher conferences at school. Back when I was in grade school and high school her lack of interest had always hurt me. I came to believe that she just wasn't interested in anything I did. It wasn't until years later that I realized she had never gone to any of Vilma's conferences either. Grandma Eutropia had always attended all of them in Mama's place. It wasn't until years later, after I got married, moved away, and started writing this book, that I finally realized Mama hadn't attended because she didn't care about me or the others—it was because she couldn't read or write. She was embarrassed to attend! After all, she hadn't gone beyond the third grade. She knows all about money, counting out change, keeping credit records, business transactions, and bartering at the markets, but she would have no idea what the teacher was talking about or trying to explain. That's why she had always sent Lola! And finally realizing that, it gave me a completely different outlook on my childhood in many respects.

CHAPTER 4

Typhoon Ruping Comes to Town

Mactan Island is normally protected against the majority of the typhoons that hit the Philippines each year. Being an inner island protected on all sides by a number of much larger isles, a direct hit is a rare event. In the second week of November of 1990, however, a raging storm so large and so powerful struck the south-central part of the country, tore through Mactan Island, and continued unabated across the entire width of the island chain nearly taking everything and everyone with it. I was 13 years old at the time. It was the year that Mom and Dad had built their dream home. They had finally been able to replace our Nipa house with one of cinder-block and wood siding, two stories high with a tin roof. We were so happy and proud!

In the typical Filipino custom not to be wasteful, we had lived in the Nipa house until the main house was completed. Then we attached the Nipa structure to the front of the house to use as a store. Mama began buying supplies and stocked her new business—Maxima's Store—with a variety of food items, snacks, daily necessities, and her best selling products: a variety of wines and San Migel beer.

Papa had been making a good living for some time. He had been fully employed as the main caretaker for the Valencia Babag fish ponds since the mid-1970s. The doctor had divided up his Cebu property holdings and had given each of his five sons ten hectars containing fish ponds when he passed away. The fish ponds in our area were inherited by Debostines Valencia and his wife, Petra. He continued employing grandpa as caretaker. By the late 1960s, however, Floro was losing his eyesight and increasingly became unable to work the ponds. As the family looks back upon it now, it is unknown what caused the condition. Perhaps it was cataracts or perhaps it was from diabetes. Some in the family even believed it was from *engkantos* or bad spirits. No one knows for sure. All we really know is that by the mid-1970s, a couple years before I was born, grandpa Floro was blind. He had suggested to Sir Valencia that his son-in-law, my father Claro, be hired in his place as he had taught him everything he knew about the business. Since Floro was well-respected in the Valencia family for his work and honesty and my father had been working with him for a number of years, Valencia hired papa and turned over full responsibility for the fish ponds to him.

Papa had been working the fish ponds for a long time. After graduating from grade school he had, at the suggestion of his Aunt, begun working for Floro Tumulak. That is where he met Maxima Tumulak, Floro's daughter who would someday become my mother. Maxima often brought them water or lunch when they were consumed with a work-project and she and Claro became good friends and, eventually, sweethearts. Mama says that Grandma Lola was always telling Claro he should marry her daughter so she could get away from Grandpa Lolo who was always beating her. With a laugh, Mama always claimed she married Papa just to get out of the house and away from the chores and taking care of her brothers and sisters. Of course, they always lived next door or somewhere close by after they were married so somehow I suspect that claim. Anyway, they were married on June 26, 1968.

Papa had the same arrangements with Debostines Valencia as Grandpa Floro had with Sir Valencia. Milk-Fish and Prawns were raised in the fish ponds for the Valencia family to sell in the markets and to the restaurants while Tilapia and shrimp were raised for my family to sell in the markets and throughout our neighborhood. That was the payment arrangement. Papa received no cash for his work but was always able to provide his family fresh seafood to eat and to make money by selling the surplus fish. During the fish harvest time, Mama would go out and sell the surplus around the neighborhood and take others to the fish market early in the mornings to sell. My Uncle Oscar further down the road, was caretaker of a kelp, or seaweed, farm with similar arrangements so he and my parents often bartered back and forth. After years of this, my parents had been able to scrimp and save enough money to construct a sturdy, nice little two-story house for their family of six children.

Over the years my parents and their growing family had endured a number of tropical storms and typhoons. I remember going through several as a little girl. Having no basement or storm-cellar as many Americans do, nor having emergency shelters established in the area by our local government, Filipinos are left to seek shelter in such storms as best as they can. We would usually huddle up in grandpa Floro's home or, as it began to fall into disrepair over the years, we would go over to Uncle Dictivo's solidly-built home of concrete and marble, to ride out most storms. Uncle Dictivo was a merchant marine, a Chief Engineer on a cargo ship that traveled the world, and he could afford a more luxurious, solidly built home. Whether he was home or not, we were always welcome to take shelter in the house with Aunt Delia and our cousins until the storm passed but we seldom did this over the years because we did not want to be a bother.

However, nothing as powerful as Typhoon Ruping had ever visited this area of my country in my lifetime nor, as we later found out, in the lifetime of my parents. From November 10 to 13 of 1990, the great typhoon was out in the ocean bearing down on the outer edges of the south central part of the Philippine Islands reaching sustained winds of 205 kph with gusts of 220kph. This powerful howler was creating huge waves, sinking ships and killing people before it ever got to land. It tore into the province of Surigao del Norte, making landfall at Dinagat Island at midnight of November 12-13 and headed for Southern Leyte. By the dawn of November 13 it was devastating Maasin and the surrounding area, uprooting trees, toppling utility poles, disintegrating houses, and bringing in tidal waves that were putting entire areas under water. By late in the afternoon, Ruping left Leyte behind as it went off into the sea but maintained all of its strength as it moved towards the Mactan-Cebu area. As news of the terrific storm sounded more and more frightening, Papa and my two older brothers left Mama and the rest of us at Uncle Dictivos as they rushed out to reinforce the levees around the fish ponds. The fish farm was always Papa's first priority during and after these storms. The aftermath of a typhoon can be very damaging to the ponds. Sometimes the water will rise from the heavy rain and if that happens then we have a huge problem to face. Similar problems are caused by tidal flooding. Whenever a large typhoon or heavy winds approached any part of the central Philippines, my father and brothers would rush over to the fish farm and build a higher dike around the ponds so when the storm hit, the fish would remain safe and not wash away or go out with the tide. To quickly build the dikes up, they would wade out along the edge of the ponds and began digging at the soft mud with their hands and throw it up onto the top of the dike to increase its height. They would have to move all along the sides and do this quickly and then pack it down to make it withstand the approaching rainstorm or flooding. During heavy storms such as this, it was quicker for Papa to be the one to wade out into the water and quickly move around the pond's shore throwing the mud up as my brothers followed along on the dike stomping and packing it down solid. Then large nets are often laid over each pond as further protection. But all of this exhausting work is no guarantee. And as we found out later, Papa was nearly killed in this storm. According to him, as the storm approached and he and the boys had gone around building up the levees, he was growing tired but hurriedly laid the nets out and began to arrange them, intending to cover the ponds to keep the fish from being washed out by the impending tidal surge and flooding. As the tremendous wind and waves increased, he missed his footing and was blown into one pond tangling him in the netting. He struggled to keep his head above water calling for help, but only saw his two young teenage sons, Carlito and Ferdinand, come up close to the water and, with wide eyes, watch him struggling under the large wet, heavy net winding around his struggling body. As the wind-driven rain pelted them unmercifully until they could no longer see and the wind and the waves increased dramatically, they found they couldn't help without endangering their own lives and frantically watched papa struggling under the net as it settled toward the bottom of the pond. The net was hundreds of meters square and quite heavy. After what seemed like minutes of holding his breath and struggling to get free Papa, nearly exhausted and ready to give-up, all of a sudden, as if by miracle, finally cleared the side of the net, swam up and broke the surface gasping for air!

That evening Ruping slammed into Mactan Island full force. Immediately, we were in total darkness. The howling wind, the noise of breaking glass, the eerie sounds of splintering wood and the frightening sound of debris swirling about outside kept us all quiet in the darkness—afraid of what might happen next.

What had seemed like such a long time finally came to an end at dawn on November 14 as the storm moved on. As we slowly emerged out into the open, we could hardly believe our eyes. Hardly anything higher than one-story existed as far as we could see and much of that was heavily damaged. All the trees as far as we could see were down or completely gone. The entire second floor of my grandparents' home and part of the back of the house's ground floor was blown away and my parents' dream house next door was completely erased. The roof was gone. Most of the second floor was ripped away. Much of the ground floor was reduced to rubble. My parents lost everything. What little they had accumulated over the years was gone. Their few appliances, our dishes, our clothes, our towels, blankets, our pictures, our books, everything. They had put all of their energy and spare time into making a nice little home for our family and Ruping had come along and turned it all into scattered piles of debris. It was a very big loss to my parents. This was the only thing they had ever wanted to see from the money that my father had made over the years during his long employment at the fish ponds. They wanted the memorabilia that would last for generations to come. Pictures and belongings to hand down to their children. Now there was only a few things that could be salvaged. My uncles' homes all around us sustained some damage too, but because they were all one-story structures they had survived total destruction—probably protected to some extent by the height of my parents' and grandparents' homes.

In the Philippines there is no insurance for such things. We couldn't afford it if it was available. And there is no government agency to come around to help you. At the same time, the people don't wander around complaining about the government's lack of help or blame the government for what happened as they do in America after such disasters. Instead, in the Philippines the people set about assessing the damage, cleaning up the mess, salvaging what they can, and getting their lives back to normal as soon as possible. This is done in every yard, in every block, in every neighborhood and among family members, relatives and neighbors all working together.

The men and older boys go about retrieving various parts of the housing that can be salvaged and making repairs while the women, with the help of their daughters and younger children, gather up the clothing and household items and furnishings that has been scattered around. Clothing is sorted, and in some cases the proper owners located in the neighborhood and turned over to them, to be washed after being scattered about in the rain and mud during the storm. The aftermath of a typhoon can be a mixed blessing. People enjoy finding things and an abundance of fruit is always available, blown down by the storm. Sometimes a family is lucky and acquires something nice or valuable, blown onto their property from somewhere unknown while at the same time a family might loose something valuable blown into a neighboring yard and just can't bring themselves to ask for it back. In the Philippines sometimes mere possession, or whose yard something landed in after a storm like this, determines who now owns it. This is often true in cases of someone's roof or wall. Because of its size and difficulty in handling, its new owner might be determined by where it landed.

Typhoon Ruping, we later learned, had been the nation's sixth most devastating in our history. It was the worst and most powerful to hit this area since 1947. The damage to power lines left most of the central Visayas without power for weeks. Telephone lines, too, were down and the entire area was cut off from the outside world. We also learned that 47 ships in and around the harbors had been sunk during the storm and nearly 46 provinces, or more than half the country, was affected. A state of Calamity—similar to a State of Emergency in the United States—was declared in 27 of those provinces as over 200,000 houses were destroyed and hundreds of hectares of rice, sugar cane, and banana crops were completely ruined. In all, it was determined that the storm had affected over one-million Filipinos directly and over five-million indirectly while nearly 1,300 were injured, nearly 750 were killed and another 740 were never found.

After Typhoon Ruping, our dream house became a legend in our family. We all want to believe the house was really there but sometimes it does seem like just a dream. It was ours to enjoy for such a short time. Every year at every family gathering someone will bring the topic up, especially when my father and brothers have had too much to drink. They reminisce and talk about what should have been. About how life, sometimes, seems so unfair and why some people seem to never have such problems with wealth and with life. But then someone among them finally remembers how blessed we were that none of our family or relatives were killed or hurt in that storm.

Typical damage caused by a typhoon passing through the island chain.

Typhoons in my country are a common occurrence. We usually have two or three a year and although they seldom hit the Cebu-Mactan area directly, we almost always sustain some kind of damage from the heavy rain or winds that accompany them. Our family built another house out of the salvaged cinder-block and wood but it was never comparable to the structure that had been destroyed by Ruping. Nearly every year afterwards, it seems, we had to repair our house from the aftermath of some lessor typhoon that had passed by somewhere. My father and two older brothers always took the responsibility of putting our house back together while my mother and us girls would do the clean up, wash all the clothing that had become soaked from the rain or flooding, find all of our housewares that sometimes would end up in our neighbors yard, and all of our other belongings. Sometimes we would have to wander around into several different yards to locate everything and sometimes we would have to ask permission to get something back. Most people would let us retrieve any item without question but there was always someone who might refuse, especially when it was one of us children trying to get it back. In those cases, we would return and tell Mama, who would then determine how best way to retrieve the item or if it was worth the trouble.

I remember that after each big storm, the adults were often very sad to learn of deaths involved or to deal with all the devastation, damage and financial problems that it caused but most of us kids were innocent and naive of all this. After the scary part of the storm was over, we kids were usually happy, including me, my two sisters and my three brothers. A typhoon usually meant no school for almost a week. In the meantime we would play in the flooded areas or swim in it, pretending it was the ocean, and we would go around and find a lot of coconut fruits, tamarine fruits, bananas, mangoes, and many, many more varieties of fruit that became abundantly available on the ground around the trees after such a storm. To this day I just can't recall of ever being sad after a typhoon—except for the day that Typhoon Ruping came to town and destroyed our dream home.

CHAPTER 5

My High School Years

My high school years turned into a bad experience. Or perhaps I should say, a worse experience. I went through all kinds of personal and emotional problems and believed that I would never have an easy life like some of my friends enjoyed. I guess, in looking back, perhaps they were just the typical teenage problems but at times I believed the storm was too strong for me to handle. I dealt with each problem by mirroring, or comparing, my life to the lives of others who seemed far worse off than me and convinced myself that I was not the only person in the world who had to toil in life and that God would never abandon me. My faith in God, in fact, comforted me in these times and made me believe that there was always hope—that behind the gathering storm clouds there was still sunlight that would eventually come out and shine to help promote new life. It was this belief that kept me going, convinced that one day I would have a good life, a good future, and that God would always watch over me.

Unfortunately, it was about this time, in my second year of high school, that we learned Papa would be forced to retire from his long-term position as the Valencia family's fish-pond caretaker. After inheriting the property from his father and operating it for a number of years, Papa's boss, Debostines Valencia, decided to sell the property because he didn't want the responsibility of the business any more. He had grown tired of all the people who were always trying to steal fish and threatening my father's life and he didn't want to take any more chances of any problems like that coming up—especially when he knew that many times my father had been in danger because of professional "fish rustlers" who had wanted to kill him. I remember many such instances over the years and I really think the job of "fishpond caretaker" that my father had is extremely dangerous in the Philippines. Some poor people are desperate and will try anything and, I guess, there is also a lucrative "black-market" in selling stolen farm-raised fish cheaply—with low overhead—in a third-world country. Gangs were sometimes even involved. Unbelievably, Papa had to carry a gun as a "fishpond caretaker." But those who tried to steal fish were also armed and occasionally shootouts actually occurred over a stupid net-full of fish! So, sometimes having such a job was really a nightmare. As a little girl I remember one night when I think we almost lost my father and my two brothers. That night a group of stealers came up and started shooting at my father and my two brothers who there with him helping out. As Papa had trained them, they all ran off in a zig-zag pattern when the shooting started and met at a specified location. Luckily some people in the area who knew Papa heard the shooting and ran off to our house and notified Mama who sent us kids after the police. When Mama and the police arrived at the fish ponds they found Papa and my two brothers all hiding at the top of a tall coconut tree. Papa said that for a time the "rustlers" had stood at the bottom of the tree shooting up at them but luckily, in the dark, they kept hitting the coconuts. Despite such dangers, my father had always insisted he loved the job and would never trade it for anything. In addition, his position of "fishpond care-taker" had provided us children so much fun and many fond memories throughout all those years that he had devoted to the job. The site had become our playground and had provided our family not only food but nearly all the resources we needed for day to day living such as wood and stones for various projects at home and sticks and brush as fuel for cooking and various other needs and necessities. In fact, the fish ponds served as our family's recreation park and provided all of our needs.

For several weeks after being informed of Valencia's decision, all Papa could do was wish and hope for the miracle that his boss would change his mind about closing the operation down. My parents really worried about this for a while because they didn't know what was going to happen to them next or what kind of job would be available to them in the future. They had purchased land from Lolo Tumulak when they married just like the others, but over the years they had sold off various small portions of it to a number of my uncles in our times of financial difficulties or in order to meet the needs of us kids or to survive in paying off debts and credit. Now they only had the land their home sat on and did not want to risk losing that. Besides their ages, neither of my parents had ever finished school and now that really scared them both. They knew they would have trouble obtaining another job. All my father knew was the fish-pond business and he had gotten that position through relatives and Mama had started her own neighborhood convenience store and street-side cafeteria but because of large credit accounts that were never paid that she had provided to our relatives, neighbors and friends, those businesses had gone into bankruptcy several times. My parents were growing scared and unsure if a new store and cafeteria business would work to really support our family. Our future was becoming a huge challenge for them and the change that was coming in our lives was a bit scary for all of us. Papa had loved this fish-pond job and never expected this to happen. Nor had he ever prepared for the possibility of it closing down.[1]

When I heard about the situation with Papa's job, I became scared too. I felt my problems would only get worse. In addition to worrying that our family would not have enough to eat, I had hardly gotten into high school and now my parents were facing all kinds of problems from left to right. I feared I would have to quit school again. Those two years I was out greatly hurt me personally and I didn't want to think of the possibility of it happening again. My two brothers, Carlito and Ferdinand, had already quit school years earlier because of the financial problems but actually, I don't think they cared, at the time, as much about education as I did. They often times did some goofy things before they dropped out. During one school day, they both skipped and didn't show up for class because they had decided to go play basketball. Another time they went swimming. And on yet another occasion they went off with some street kid to hunt for some wild fruit like guava, mango and coconuts, and were gone all day. My parents desperately wanted the boys to finish school. Papa and Mama knew from experience how important it would be for them as head of their families after they got married. My parents figured it was less important for Helen or me because in our country, at that time anyway, women could get along okay by simply taking care of the chores in the home. Today, of course, it is an entirely different matter. But I understand why my parents weren't as concerned about my education, at the time, as I was. I can even remember one time my mother criticizing my work of clothes washing, telling me my whites would never pass! She gave me all kinds of words about it at the time and embarrassed me in front of a number of our neighbors. "You need more practice," she told me, "because when you get married your husband will kick you out because of your poor work!" Of course everyone laughed who overheard it except for me.

By my second year of high school Ferdinand had already re-entered school and had taken a placement test that verified his overall knowledge similar to an American G.E.D. test. Those results had placed him several grades ahead and he continued doing good. By this time school had become important to him and he enjoyed it very much. School had also become important to Carlito as well but out of necessity he continued to work in construction whenever possible in order to help out the family. Toward the end of my second year of high school I, too, took a placement test that would allow me to skip my third year of high school and go directly into my final year toward graduation.

My teacher, Mrs. Augusto, had talked me into it and convinced me I was smart enough to succeed. All the while we were growing up, my parents had always told us kids that the Tuko lizard was sacred and was not to be killed. Back then every home in the Philippines had lizards, at least the geckos or house lizards. It's not unusual for homes in the tropics to have lizards waddling up the wall or across the ceiling. Today, houses are being constructed much more tight or secure but back then most houses didn't have screens over their windows, just the wood slats that we would open or close for privacy. Many older homes in tropical regions are still like that. So flies pass in and out during the day and mosquitos at night. The lizards soon follow. In the Philippines there are about 100 species of lizards, none of which are poisonous. The most common is the gecko or house lizard. These are anywhere from about an inch to five inches long and they often gathered around a ceiling light. I guess they were territorial because I seldom ever saw more than one gecko at each lightbulb throughout the house. You seldom ever saw them in the daytime, but in the evening as we watched TV or ate our meal, the little creatures would come out and wait patiently near the bulb for the insects attracted to the light to pass near. The little geckos would usually catch more of the flying insects than would get away. That is probably why lizards in the house are considered good luck in the Philippines. And while having house lizards was considered a good fortune, having a Tuko, a lizard nearly a foot long, in the house was considered the best luck of all! Even though as a little girl I was afraid of the Tuko, I remember several occasions over-hearing my papa, in the other room, asking the Tuko the winning numbers he should pick in *Jai-Alai*, a game conducted in the Philippines similar to the lottery in America but with smaller numbers and jackpots. In fact, adults all across the Philippines, in addition to my parents, often asked all kinds of things of the giant lizard because they believed it could predict the future accurately by how many times it answered "Tu-ko" upon hearing your question. As time went on as I was growing up, my parents asked the Tuko many things and Papa would constantly ask for the winning numbers. Then, I too became the tuko's fan after I acquired a number of pen-pals and began asking him every day if I would be receiving a letter in the next day's mail.

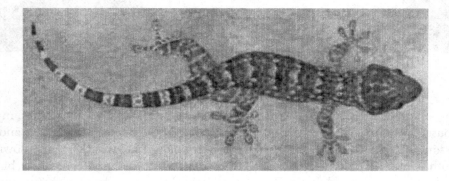

There were many beliefs regarding the Tuko.

I guess times were becoming difficult for all of us, even the Tuko. By my second year of high school Papa had become desperate for some financial help and although the Tuko could provide us the good fortune of eliminating the insects from our house, it was never able to provide Papa the good luck he needed to win the *Jai-Alai* jackpot. In fact, it seemed the Tuko that lived in our house wasn't bringing much luck to us at all. Our family was going through a long period of tough times by then with Papa being forced into his retirement and Mama's store going bankrupted not just once, but three different times, and me going through all the problems of a typical teenager.

Me in my turbulent teen years.

I fretted about being poor. By my teen years appearances—my clothes, my house, my family and my looks—were becoming of the upmost importance and, in some cases, an embarrassment. Not only was I required to wear hand-me-down clothes from my older sisters, and in some cases even from my older brothers, but I was also dark skinned. In the Philippines, light skin is considered very attractive and is a sign of beauty, wealth, success, and a higher class of people. It is believed that dark skinned people are unattractive, that they work outside in the sun at menial jobs and are poorer. To us it is quite simple. The lighter the skin, the more rich and successful the person. Poor hardworking people are very dark. Most of our movie and TV stars are very light. Ironically, while American Caucasians might be paying money to get tanned and brown, Filipinos are paying money for skin-whitening agents and creams to get light or white. And in my teenage mind, it was hard to get respect and to be well-liked by my peers and others if I had dark brown skin. Having lighter skin was becoming more important with each passing day.

Being even more poor by this time, of course, I couldn't afford the skin-lighting creams and soaps such as Likas-Papaya, Lux Bioderm and other brands that were available in the big stores to so many others. But our most popular clothes-whitening soaps at the time were Perla and Superwheel and although these were actually soaps for washing clothes, many people like my family would use them as a bath soap too. They would cost anywhere from forty- to fifty-peso per bar when a small bar—about the size that are provided Americans in hotels all across America—normally sold for around two to four pesos. But these more expensive soaps dissolved more slowly and didn't break up so easily so we would use it for washing ourselves as well as our clothes. I had always hoped that since they made clothes white, they would help whiten my skin. One problem, however, was that Perla could only be used on the face and body. If that soap got into your hair it would make it hard or stiff and stick together. Superwheel, on the other hand, was OK for hair, but regular shampoo and bath soaps were expensive and we just could not afford them as often. Perla, then, had to be used with extra care when used as a bath soap but we often used these clothes-washing bars, instead. Once in a while we could get nice *sabon homot*—creamy and good-smelling soaps and shampoos such as Ivory, Camey, Safeguard and the like—but only once in a blue moon. Unknown to my parents, however, my older sister Vilma—who always knew the latest beauty tips—had told me about a co-worker of hers who had used chlorine bleach to help lighten her skin. One day, while getting ready for school, I took a packet of mama's chlorine bleach into grandpa's outhouse and poured some of it into a bucket of water I was using for my bath. If it made mama's laundry white, I figured, then it should lighten my skin, and if Vilma's friend did it without any problems, it must be safe to use. I had also heard a rumor that Michael Jackson, my favorite American singer and dancer at the time, had a special place to go where he would lighten himself with a bleach-wash of his body and that once in a while he would rest or lay in that place for a few hours to continue the process and to help preserve his youthfulness. So that really helped my belief too, because he had become so light. I often wished I could do as he did—lay in a chlorine bath—but that, again, was just a false childish fantasy that I had heard about or had created in my teenage mind. I hid away in the outhouse and scrubbed my body all over with the bleach. Wanting quick results, sometimes I added more bleach to the water or at other times I just used less water to make it more effective. Many times my eyes were watering and I could hardly breathe as I dressed and came out of the CR. Coughing from the fumes, I looked around and determined that mama was still in the house and quickly walked over to the pile of wash and put the remainder of the packet back near the tub where mama had left it. On a number of occasions as I walked into the house to get my school books Mama, at the sink would turn and ask, "Why do you smell like chlorine?" Sometimes I would say I had menstruation and I had to wash out my underwear. She would let that go and didn't question me any further but I could only use that excuse just so many times. On other occasions I would began to stutter at her question and she would say, "You used too much in your white clothes again didn't you?" And I would say, "Uhuh. Yes I did. Your bad luck—I'm very wasteful." She would then begin to lecture me and ridicule me but her hurtful words didn't affect me at all. I was more concerned with becoming white and for a while in the following days I would just use less chlorine in the water as I continued my morning ritual hidden away in my grandfather's CR. I was determined to hide my actions from my family to avoid any of them making fun of me but I was convinced that I would be prettier if I was whiter. However, I began to grow tired of the ritual because I didn't see any improvement—except that I was probably feeling cleaner than the bathroom bowl.

After Papa's forced retirement we became dependent on the success of our family business but many times over my teen years Mama and Papa's little store suffered bankruptcy. This was because many of Mama's customers were allowed too much credit and then they either ran away or quit coming by. Such customers included many of our relatives, family friends, neighbors, and even some strangers. Many of Mama's 14 brothers and sisters had acquired much more credit at the store than they could handle but how can you tell your own brothers and sisters "NO" when they need food or help? Mama and Papa went through this several different times as they operated our little family store and each time they were taken advantage of by some of their friends and some of my Uncles or Aunts. It is sad that such people are given credit out of love and friendship but then end up your enemy. They will quarrel with you over prices, credit, or bills until you get mad enough and finally lose interest in begging them to pay. Some people say their credit can credit can be used as their burial expenses. Of course, as I look back I also think me and some of my brothers and sisters were just as responsible for the business failures because of our constant stealing of food and snacks and spending money.

Mama, and all other neighborhood small-store owners, were required to pay cash to the various truck drivers for their weekly deliveries of the few staples and convenience items, snacks, Coca Cola, and San Miguel beer that they kept in stock. Sometimes in order to do this we would acquire what was called "Turka Credit," a private loan so-called because the lady who walked around the neighborhoods providing such loans was of Turkish descent. These loans were big business. Referred to as a "5-6 loan," a store owner was allowed to borrow five-thousand pesos and then required to pay back six-thousand. Every day the loan-lady circulated through many of our communities carrying her leather "bank" bag from which she would issue her loans to the small businesses. As long as her loans were repaid in a timely manner there was never any trouble. The amount to be repaid increased with each late payment. I think, over time Mama acquired somewhere around five or six Turka Loans to keep her store running. In addition, Mama stocked her little business daily with fresh eggs, fruits, vegetables and dried fish by purchasing from neighborhood vendors each morning. Such daily purchases were usually made with cash but sometimes it became necessary to use credit here too. Our Mama, however, was kind. Sometimes too kind for a good business woman. She gave our neighbors too much credit as well as all of our relatives who asked for it. And some of our relatives would come from all over—sometimes passing by a number of closer stores—in order to buy from our Mama on credit. So Mama was often unable to pay off her credit until those who owed her paid theirs. And sometimes some of those people didn't worry quite so much about their credit as much as our Mama worried about ours.

I remember a few occasions growing up when Mama had to quickly close down her store—close and lock down the shutters over the windows and counters and hide in the house with us kids—when she heard the "Turka" was in the neighborhood collecting. There were other times—after she had asked some patrons several times to pay their credit and had become too embarrassed to ask them again—when she would send me and Richein out to collect.

I know now it was because she was too embarrassed or ashamed to go out and plead with her own brothers and sisters for the repayment and wanted to avoid any arguments. At the time, however, me and Richein greatly resented her sending us out on these weekly collection details. People would sometimes hide from us when they saw us coming, too. At other times they would stay in their house and let their dog deal with us. Several times Richein and I were chased down the street by someone's dog who owed Mama money. Another time we were attacked by a mean turkey. The owners sat in their house and laughed as they watched the turkey chase us around their yard nipping at our butts before we could finally get far enough away and run down the street. It was especially difficult for us when she sent us out to collect from our aunts and uncles—being that we were family, and their little nephew and niece at that—they often found it easy to be not only rude, but sometimes just down-right nasty about it! After I and Richein walked up and I would say what we had been instructed to say—"Mama sent us to ask if you would please pay your credit"—one aunt and uncle would always begin to argue among themselves over who had credited anything at the store. Their argument would continue to get louder and more and more escalated until Richein and I got scared and ran off. As I look back I think, maybe, that was their tactic to get out of paying because they would *always* do that. Then there were others who would tell Richein and me to go home and not to worry about their credit because they had so much money they didn't know what to do with it all or they might even give it to our parents and buy us kids so that we would have to stay with them. Still others would hand us a check and say, "Here! See if your parents can cash this." Richein and I hated to be sent out on these collection errands. So many of Mama's customers acted as if we were the bad people.

Of course, there were also times that we were short on cash and Mama would send me out to borrow money from one of my aunts to go buy a coconut or to ask for a coconut. I found this extremely embarrassing too. Instead, on my way to one of my aunt's houses, usually my Aunt Seding, I would wander around the neighborhood trying to find a good coconut that had fallen to the ground. I would return home and tell Mama, "Here, Aunt Seding said we could have this one."

Credit and debit problems at home and at the store were causing more and more problems as time went on which created more and more problems in our home and in our family. My parents were always on edge and arguing nearly all the time during this period. Papa and my older brothers did occasionally get temporary jobs in construction but we had become more and more dependent on the little store and I would lay in bed at night and hear my parents argue in the other room. I would get sad upon hearing all of this and began to cry and worry about what was going to happen to my once happy family. Many times during this period I cried myself to sleep. It helped somewhat when Mama leased the store out, but it still didn't take care of all of our financial problems or provide us with all our needs. Besides, once she leased the store out anything we now needed or wanted from the store, we had to pay for up-front.

It was also around this time, when I was 17, that I and my brothers and sisters found out that our Papa was being unfaithful to our mama and was seeing another women. We were devastated. Our family, our world, was deteriorating right in front of us. Mama was angry. I was angry. We were all angry. Sometimes Mama would threaten to run away. Sometimes Mama and Papa would argue and then Mama would go off and hide behind the house or go stay at one of our Aunts' homes to make Papa or us worry. It led to more arguments between Mama and Papa which led to more arguments between me and Papa and the rest of the family. Slowly, he and Mama tried to work things out between them.

On August 24 of 1994 another blow hit me that greatly affected my life. That day Fernando Tumulak, my favorite Uncle, was found dead floating in the channel beneath the Mactan Island-Mandaue City Bridge. I never realized until I looked back on it years later that Uncle Fernando was Gay. I guess that is why he always knew so much about fashion, dancing, makeup, and had been so good at organizing our Miss Universe games. As we grew older he worked with our hair and taught us girls how to wear makeup. But being Gay in the Philippines back then was a huge slap in the face and a great embarrassment to our family and to my other uncles—his brothers. Several of them were always beating him up—I guess to beat the Gay out of him. It never worked.

Neither the police nor our family could ever determine if Uncle Fernando had committed suicide or if someone had killed him because he was Gay. His death hurt me deeply. I loved him very much. He was so-o-o kind to everyone and went out of his way to help other people and to help entertain us kids. He never did anything to hurt any body. Again, life seems so unfair sometimes but we have to learn to live with it.

It was about this time that my Papa and I began to engage in a show of wits. I knew my Papa's habits, studied him, and began to learn his secrets. I and the other kids would watch him to make sure he wasn't being unfaithful again to our mother. In addition, I would study his movements and know when he had money, what he was doing with it, and where he kept it. Often times after he had done odd jobs for someone and had gotten paid, he would turn some of his pay over to Mama for the family and stash some of it away for himself or perhaps for future needs. Sometimes Mama would later ask him for some money and he would tell her he didn't have any and I would say, "He's lying Mama. I saw him hide some in the rafters" and then they would get into another argument. After a while, he would look all around to make sure I wasn't watching him from somewhere and then try to find a new hiding place. He tried a variety of ingenious locations. Once he stuffed it inside his flashlight and once he put it inside the back of our radio. Sometimes it worked and sometimes I would try and determine where he might hide his money and then search and find it. It almost became like a game. I also learned whenever I needed money for snacks or for a school project it was best to wait until he had a few drinks. Before, whenever I asked Papa for money, like Mama he would tell me he was sorry but he didn't have any. But then I would see him having a drink and snacks with his barkadas—friends—and I would wait a little while, walk up again and ask, and he would give me the money I needed. Sometimes he would give me more than I needed and at other times I would just simply ask for more than was required for the project! After a while I became really good at this manipulation as well as constantly being able to find his stash of money. Papa became quite frustrated at this and was forever trying to out-smart me but he never became angry about it.[2]

One evening during my second year of high school a remarkable event happened. The end of the school year was only a week away. As Richein and I sat in our living room watching TV, an orange butterfly fluttered through the open door and all around the room before it ventured back outside. We Filipinos have a belief about butterflies in the house, too. A black one flying into the house is a sign of an impending death in the family, a yellow butterfly signifies that we will have a visitor or someone in the house will be receiving money, and an orange one foretells of someone in the house receiving an important letter. In other words, gray, black and brown butterflies are a bad sign while the light or bright colors are a good luck sign that brings hope. The following day at school, at approximately 4:30 p.m., the students in all grades were gathering in line for the end-of-the-day flag ceremony. Like the morning event, this too is a daily school activity to show respect for our flag. Different students are assigned each day to raise the banner in the morning or to lower the banner in the afternoon. Those assigned to the lowering of the flag take it off and fold it very gently as the remainder of the school body quietly watches and then they put it in the place where it belongs. I was in the line waiting for the teacher to start. While standing there, I noticed someone touching me on my arm. The first time I ignored it because I thought it might just be a male classmate who wanted my attention. Then I heard a little voice whispering in my ear saying, "I have a letter!" Then I realized it was my brother Richein. I looked around at him and smiled. I could tell he was excited. A young boy who was very happy and excited. Then, because of his reaction, my heart began to pump very fast. I finally realized that the letter he referred to was for me! To make certain, I whispered, "Who's letter? Where did it come from?" And he excitedly blurted out, "It's a pen pal of yours!" Unable to contain myself, I demanded, "From where?" and he handed me the letter and said, "From the U.S.A.!" Ignoring our flag ceremony, but quickly realizing we should quiet down, I looked at the envelope and remained silent. I couldn't believe it. My heart was full of joy having received this letter. I reacted with so much joy. I hugged my brother and thanked him for delivering the good news. We held hands tightly, whispering back and forth during the ceremony. We both wanted to shout out our happiness. We were so excited and proud and we both wanted everyone to know that I now had an American man friend! It was a big deal back then among all of us Filipinos or at least it seems like it was—perhaps it was just in my own imagination in those days. But this was my very first letter! I had never received a letter from another country before—not even my parents had, that I can ever recall. Because of this, the darkness I saw in my life seemed to gradually disappear that day and I saw a tiny light of hope showing me to have faith. My mom was a little happy that day too when I arrived home and showed it to her. I know mom was so proud that someone had written a letter to one of her daughters. I can't explain it, but I felt differently toward her that day too. I believed this was the beginning and realization of my dream. Just this one letter created a whole new episode—a whole new outlook—in my life. It was just what I needed after the tragedies of my uncle's death, my father's betrayal, my parents arguing, the store bankruptcy, the uncertain future of my continuing of school, and everything else that seems to have culminated during my second year of high school. The letter brought hope to my uncertain future. In addition, a few days later I learned that, like Ferdinand, I too passed the placement test—thanks to my teacher Mrs. Augusto for her help in seeing it through. Without her suggestions or convincing of me to take the test, maybe I would not have finished school. It seemed, at the time, my life was getting worse by then and although I was close enough to get my high school diploma, I was nearly ready to just give up and succumb to whatever life was to give me. I remember being very happy upon Mrs. Augusto informing me of the results of that test. It meant that Ferdinand and I wouldn't have to quit school again because we were close enough to finishing and my parents could manage until we completed our education and got jobs.

With the arrival of this first letter, it seemed my life was getting exciting. After being told for so long that I was short, ugly and had a wide flat nose, I was glad someone was interested in writing me. I had included my photo with my letters to the potential pen-pals so they knew what I looked like and they were still interested. And since that first letter came and I was now going to enter my Senior year of high school, my parents had changed their attitude about me too. Or so it seemed to me, anyway.

Chapter 6

A Pen-Pals' Life

The letter was a great and wonderful surprise to my entire family. One morning, several months before his death, Uncle Fernando had stopped by our house and asked me if I was *really* interested in having a foreign pen-pal. We all knew Uncle Fernando had several foreign pen-pals that he had been writing for some time. I told him I honestly wanted a pen-pal from the USA so he told me to give him 20-peso by the following morning as he would be going into Cebu City and he would register my name with an agency there. The following morning I gave him the P20 when he stopped by on his way into the city. It was money I had saved back along with some additional I had borrowed from my parents. Weeks and then months passed, and then his death, without ever hearing any more about it. We had just assumed Uncle Fernando must have used the money for himself while he was on one of his trips into the city. My Aunt Aling, his own sister, seemed to have even confirmed it. She had later told me and my family that she had once given him money to register her for an American pen-pal, too, but since she had never received any letters she was sure he had just used her money for himself. But the arrival of this letter proved once and for all that our Uncle Fernando had been falsely accused. He had been sincere and had kept his word after all.

After school Richein and I rushed home to show it to everyone and to read it out loud for our whole family to hear. It was a big, wonderful deal! The letter was from a man named Dale, who owned a large acreage with a log cabin outside of the city of Charlotte in the state of North Carolina. After the letter was read and we had all talked about it for a while, I took it out to our neighbor from across the street, Binigno Monet, who was sitting in Mama's café having a cold beer and his favorite dish, a plate of Mama's fried eggplant. Binigno was a transplanted New York American who had lived in our neighborhood for a number of years. He had become a good friend to my parents and to our whole family. Because he liked Mama's cooking, he often patronized her café and had always treated us kids kindly. He often said that the Avenido kids where the most polite and well-behaved children in the whole neighborhood and, knowing my interest, he had often talked to me about America whenever he was at our store or café. When I came out and showed him the letter he was very happy for me. He told me people from North Carolina were all good people and for the remainder of the afternoon he sat there and told me as much as he knew about the state and about its people.

Dale and I wrote back and forth for some time but he kept offering to send me a plane ticket to come visit him. My parents were not impressed with this suggestion because they believed that if a man truly loved and cared for a girl, and had some respect for her, then he would be interested and willing to come to her place to meet her parents and family. In fact, it is a common belief to Filipinos that it is the woman's place to stay put and let the man come to her and make the first move. Most Filipino girls are very humble and not aggressive at all. In conservative Filipino society, the girls are often looked-after and chaperoned where ever they go, even during a simple visit to a person of the opposite sex sitting in her own yard. When I took Dale's letter out to our neighbor Binigno Monet, who was sitting at a table in our own yard, my brother Richein accompanied me and sat nearby as Binigno and I talked about America. One of my parents or brothers was *always* with me where ever I went as I got older. Before that—when I was younger—it was always one of my older sisters or parents. So, needless to say, my mother and father insisted I was not to accept Dale's offer or even think about the possibility of going to meet him in America. I thought I was in love with him but, although I was curious about the USA, I had no desire to fly over there by myself to visit or stay with him.

In the meantime, after being allowed to skip the third year of high school I had a rough time during my senior year with the various lessons but, although they were difficult for me, I managed to survive. Of course, it also helped having a new outlook on life with my new American pen-pal.

In order to cover the cost of my graduation gown and other fees, Papa and Mama had to sell off several bags of fertilizer left over from the fish farm operation and some of our appliances, including our refrigerator, and other things. When Ferdinand graduated a year later, they had to sell off the remainder of our kitchen appliances and Mama, in order to get some additional cash, even rented out our storefront to a family friend to operate.

After I graduated, I wasted no time in applying for work. I had heard that a lot of my classmates already had a job waiting for them after graduation. Many in my class, in fact, were always very ambitious. At least many of those who graduated with me in March of 1995. I went out and applied at several different companies. However, filing applications for employment in the Philippines is very different than it is in the United States. In the Philippines, companies do not have or hand out applications. Such forms must be purchased by perspective applicants at a store—such as a Variety Store or a Stationary Store. In addition, each applicant is required to submit a recent photograph—similar to a passport photo—with that application. So with each submission to each company, it costs the job seeker a substantial amount of money for the form and the cost of a photo. This might range anywhere from two pesos for the form and 25-peso for a photograph along with the cost of transportation—both to and from the photo studio and to the company to turn in your application. Unlike in America, the application is not turned in to the company's personnel department but to the security guard at the front gate. If there is not a picture attached to the form or the security guard, for some reason, does not like you or does not think you are pretty enough, he will throw your application into the trash as soon as you walk away. In the Philippines, I guess, nothing is free so applications are not filed frivolously and not getting a job that was applied for costs the family money. Still, great crowds often gather for a few meager positions.

On one particular dramatic occasion that I remember, during an "open" or direct hiring of a certain number of people who were going to be interviewed that day for one company, the crowd surged forward in anticipation as the company's front gates were opened and I was nearly trampled and crushed in the process. In this particular case, there was a limited number of positions to be filled and numbers were being handed out to the crowd for a chance to take the company's qualification tests. My cousin Marebel and I went there together that day to try and get two of those positions. There was a big turnout of several hundred people, if not a thousand, who were apparently desperate to get jobs too. Marebel and I had gotten there early and we were near the front of the crowd. As the gates opened, everyone rushed forward like a bunch of stampeding animals with no respect for anybody. That day I saw true desperation on many of my countrymen's faces. I could have been killed and no one running over me would have cared or even noticed. Being smaller than the majority there, I was pushed forward uncontrollably within the crowd, lost my shoe, fell down, and was nearly trampled. In fact, I would have probably been trampled to death if I hadn't been able to get back on my feet. To this day I do not know how I managed to get back up while the mass was moving forward. It was just by the Grace of God, I guess. Marebel had been unable to help me. We had become separated as she, too, had been pushed and propelled forward by the surging crowd.

After I had filed a number of applications, I returned home to Mama's complaints that I was wasting what little money the family had on my "pie-in-the-sky" job applications. In the following weeks, while waiting on any telegrams from the companies where I had applied, I helped my mom in her little convenience store and cafeteria and, of coarse, in doing lots of house work. In my country, once a sufficient number of applications have been filed, we then have to wait for the various companies to notify us by telegram or courier to come in on a certain date to take their entrance or qualification exam. Once that is passed, we are called back to take a dexterity test. If that is also passed, we are then notified to come in for a personal interview. Succeeding that, and we are hired, they send us to get a medical exam to make sure we are physically fit and then the last step in the Filipino hiring process is to wait to be notified of a start date after passing what we refer to as "an FBI" which, in America, is just referred to as a background check In the Philippines these background investigations are done by the company's security guards or by a local policeman hired by the company. In addition to checking police records in your area to determine if you have ever been in serious trouble, they circulate around your neighborhood and ask questions to see what the neighbors know and think about you. The entire hiring process, including all of these various stages, can take a month or two once an application has been filed with any company.

In the meantime, one morning my aunt in-law's niece Ayon convinced me to go with her to nearby Mandaue City to apply for another job. She had found an interesting ad in the newspaper and showed it to me. I didn't pay so much attention to the full text of the ad but what really got my quick notice was the "200-peso-a-day" claim in it and the assertion that we didn't even need a highschool background as long as we were willing to learn the job and could speak good English. That seemed too good to be true and we didn't want to take the chance of losing any opportunity to a large crowd, so off we went.

I also saw this as a great opportunity to practice my speaking and reading of English and to help me gain independence from my family by becoming more self reliant. Since writing to Dale, I had heard Americans would be reluctant to marry a Filipina if she wasn't completely fluent in reading and writing English like a professional. It was important for me to impress my pen-pal when I met him.

We paid a driver for transportation directly to the site and when we got there we learned it wasn't even necessary to have an application or provide any personal information to the company. They immediately assigned us to an individual trainer who was to take us out and teach us what they called "sales marketing"—or what we found out was simply a fancy name for direct door to door sales. We had a number of different items to offer such as books, lotions, powders, and other such things. Ayon was assigned to a young man to be trained and I was assigned to a girl. Then, all of us were loaded into a van and driven out to various neighborhoods to be dropped off to begin selling. Ayon and I became separated. I didn't like that much. I was nervous. Ayon was a college graduate who had a lot more experience about being out in strange neighborhoods and I wasn't even sure how to get back home by myself. In addition, she was dressed appropriately for this kind of work while I was wearing a long dress and borrowed high heels. Although some potential customers got mad that we were bothering them, my companion and I eventually sold two books that morning and I was beginning to enjoy the job and thought, perhaps, I might like "sales marketing" after all. It was my first job outside working at Mama's store. But then later that day we went up to one house and an angry drunk man came to the door. Not only was he mad about being bothered by salesmen, but he started to chase us down the street. When he came out of his house he had something in his hand. I never did see what it was. It made no difference. All I knew was he was drunk and he was mad. That's really all that mattered. I immediately turned and I ran. Even in a dress and high heels, I outran my companion who was dressed in blue jeans and tennis shoes. Finally, after seeing no one chasing behind her, I stopped several blocks away to let her catch up with me. It was then that I decided this job was just too dangerous. Although we tried afterwards, we made no other sales throughout the remainder of the day. Perhaps because we had lost all of our confidence and had begun to approach everyone quite timidly after that incident. When that drunk man had come out of his house, I truly believed I was going to be killed. I had never had an experience with a stranger like that before.

Later that night, at 7:00 p.m., the company van came back through the neighborhood to pick us all up. I learned that Ayon was nowhere to be found and then found out that she had quit and went home around noon. I began to cry because I didn't know how I was going to get home. I had little money, most of it having been spent on lunch and supper, and I didn't know how to direct the cab drivers all the way from Mandaue City to my house. Then too, I was too upset in order to think straight enough to figure it out. I had heard on the news before about lone women being raped by their taxi driver and I didn't want to be taking the chance of traveling alone. My co-workers tried to comfort me as we rode back to the company office. We still had to sit through a post-sales pep rally to celebrate everyone's achievements for the day. Later, a boy who sold the most that day got to ring the company bell at the gathering.

Meanwhile, my parents and my brothers were out looking for me. I later learned that when Ayon arrived home, my Mama later looked her up and asked her where I was. She told Mama she didn't know, told her about the sales job, about being dropped off throughout Mandaue, and about how she and her trainer had been dropped off and had gone into the S.M. Mall and had began approaching the shoppers and various store staff making sales pitches. Apparently the Mall authorities had called the police and when they arrived, Ayon and her companion had been arrested for soliciting, taken to the police station and had finally gotten back to the company office and had quit. Although Ayon was still crying about now having a police record, Mama was furious with her and had Ayon and the whole family out looking for me in Mandaue City. As I came out of the sales meeting I heard Richein calling my name. He and Ayon had found me and had began notifying the others. Returning home that night, I was also disappointed to have learned that after all of this, we didn't even get the 200-peso per day salary. All sales had been on commission and only the *potential* was there to make P200 per day. There was no commission for us on only two sales. I don't even think the boy who got to ring the bell at that meeting had made more than a few peso.

I continued to work for Mama in her store and to help out with her cafeteria operation over the following months in the hope I would hear from one of the companies at which I had applied. Finally, in February 1996, I received a telegram from the Cebu Micro Electronics Corporation, a Japanese-owned computer-chip manufacturing company on Mactan Island, to come in for an exam. This company was located in the Mactan Export Processing Zone, commonly referred to as MEPZ but what Americans would commonly refer to as an Industrial Park, where my sister Vilma worked with Pentax. My cousin, Marebel, who had also applied at Cebu Electronics with me, received a telegram too so we went there together the following day. Apparently passing all of their tests, we were both contacted about a week later to come in for interviews. Following that, the company hired both of us and I started a week later, on March 18, working as an "Assembler" with a nine-month probationary period. Within a few months, though, I had worked my way up to the position of "Inspector" in the Quality Control division and was taken off the assembly line.

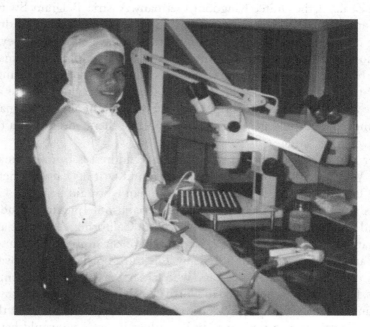

Me at work as a Quality Control Inspector at
Cebu Micro Electronics Corporation.

Every day at dawn Papa would bring water into the house for my bath and fixed me breakfast while Mama began the wash. Then Papa would fix my lunch to take to work. This usually consisted of a little fish and square of rice all wrapped up together in a little plastic bag. Sometimes when Vilma and I were working the same shift, she would come by the house to get me and off to work we would go together, catching a trike or jeepney at the main road. Eventually Papa or one of my brothers began escorting me to work because Vilma had began calling in "sick" or calling in with various excuses that she couldn't come to work at Pentax until she finally lost her job and no longer worked there. Still later, I would go off to work along with one of my friends and co-workers who would come by the house on the way.

One day, because of my continued interest and talk in eventually meeting an American man, my Aunt Salora took me to an small agency called "Hands Across the Pacific" in Cebu City. Auntie Salora had intended to help me place an ad requesting foreign pen-pals—the cost of which was to be somewhere around twenty to forty pesos for the ad along with my picture—but by the time we got there we were informed the agency was closing. The company's magazine, *Peals of the Orient*, is made available to girls throughout the Philippines and is then distributed to single men by subscription membership in many areas of Australia and New Zealand, the United Kingdom, Germany, Austria, Belgium, Switzerland, Canada, and the USA. I was disappointed we had arrived too late. I didn't know when we could ever return or when I might again have enough money. Before we left, however, the receptionist pointed to a stack of pamphlet-style magazines on a nearby table and advised that they were extra past issues of their magazine, a year or two old. She invited me to take a few home saying, "There are men who have advertised in there [for pen-pals]. Some might already be married or are no longer interested but you can write some of them and give it a try," so I took a few copies home.

Later that evening I picked five names and addresses from the magazines to write. Vilma, being more fluent in reading and writing English, helped me compose the letters. The first I picked was a man who said he was a Catholic. That was very important to me. There was a handsome picture included with his ad and it said he was a college professor from California. Another handsome photo that got my attention was a Highway Engineer from California who was divorced and had custody of his little baby. The third I picked to write was a man named Lonnie Speer, also divorced and who said he was a retired policeman from St. Louis, Missouri, who now lived in North Carolina. I do not know why I chose him because there was no picture and that really disappointed me. At the same time, my parents warned me not to write to him because he would have a gun and might be too dangerous. So the next man I chose to write was a 61-year-old man in a wheelchair. Vilma and the rest of my family joked and pointed out this was probably the best choice because if he proved to be too mean, I could always push him down a flight of stairs or off over a cliff. Looking at the other photos included with the various ads, I also chose to write to a man named Alan in North Carolina who said he was a tool-kit salesman. All of us Filipinos hear a lot about California, Hollywood, and L.A. and nearly everyone knows someone who has some relative living in that state, so a handsome man from there was an easy choice. Perhaps I chose Lonnie and Alan because their ads got my attention with the North Carolina addresses and having in my mind what Binigno Monet had told me about North Carolina people. I really don't know why I chose the people that I did except that four of the five were accompanied by handsome photos and all of their descriptions and their listed interests sounded interesting. The next day Vilma went with me to mail the letters off. Luckily, by not placing an ad in the agency's magazine, I had enough money to pay for the postage. The cost of the long distance international postage, having my little photo inside, was P10 for each envelope. This is quite expensive for us considering the normal cost of a letter is about P2 but I was very pleased and happy upon sending them off. In the following days and then the following weeks, however, it began to feel like it had been a waste of time and money. After several weeks had passed, most of the family had forgotten all about the letters and never brought the subject up again while Mama, on the other hand, thought I was foolish for having sent them and "wasting" my money in the first place and, every once in a while, reminded me about it.

Many pen-pal men, we were often told, prefer that the girls write to them first. They believed that they were better at answering a letter than at composing one. Perhaps they are shy, embarrassed, or don't know what to write. The girls on the other side of the world experience the same kind of problems. We are shy and not necessarily proficient in English. We are writing a stranger and can only hope he is someone trustworthy who is decent and will treat us with respect. We want to create a good image, create a good impression, and yet maintain our own personality and integrity. Not all of us are highly educated or have good penmanship so, sometimes letter writing is time-consuming as we take our time writing plainly and looking up words in our English dictionary in order to spell correctly and to use the right grammar. That is why I was so lucky to have Vilma. She was highly proficient both in English and in letter-writing and was more than willing to help me as long as I did work for her, and later to give me guidance as I did my own letters.

The publication, *Pearls of the Orient*, is published and distributed throughout the Cebu province. Similar publications exist in other parts of the islands, such as *Asian Rose, Hands Across the USA, Cherry Blossoms, Pacific Romance, Pacific Island Ladies, The Philippine Friendship Service*, and a number of others. Every girl who has her picture published in the little pamphlet-style booklets receive a free copy of that booklet along with another in which foreign men have placed personal ads. Generally, there are over 300 photos displayed on some 30-plus pages in the booklets. In the publications supplied to the men, only photos & first names of the girls are included, along with their ages, physical descriptions, and a four to five line paragraph about their current employment and interests. The girls' mailing addresses are provided only to subscribers upon special request and additional payment. The mailing addresses of the men are provided to the girls directly in the ads.[1] These operations are basically no different than the typical match-making services, computer-dating web-sites and personal-ad publications found and promoted throughout the United States—except these in the Philippines circulate internationally instead of locally.

Sometimes months pass without an answer to a letter or ad. There are many reasons why a person will not answer our letters. They might not have liked the picture or it didn't come out clearly in the publication, they might have become too busy since placing their ad, they might have changed their mind about having a foreign pen-pal, might be already writing someone else, or perhaps the initial letter created a bad impression such as poor penmanship, too many words spelled wrong, looked too messy, or was too strongly worded, too personal, or a host of other reasons. That is why doing our best in something as simple as writing a letter is so important. Since then I have also learned that there is a delay of anywhere from 30 to 90 days between the time an ad and photo are submitted to the time they are published and distributed. In addition, for some reason a letter sent from the Philippines to the United States takes about one week to ten days for delivery but a letter sent from the United States to the Philippines takes around 21 days and sometimes more.

Finally I received a letter in response to those I had sent out. The first letter was from the man named Alan who lived in the state of North Carolina. He seemed very nice and wrote a very polite and kind letter. As before, I shared the correspondence with my entire family. In Filipino society, such is expected. Because of our strong kinship ties, everyone in the family wants to have some say, some influence, in each other's affairs, especially in romance, and we always strive to get our family's approval. For me to receive a letter from a man is considered a family affair needing family attention and participation. I am expected to seek their approval even before any formal courtship would ever begin. To do otherwise would be considered conceded. So parents, brothers and sisters and even my aunts all had an opinion about which pen-pals were best. Who I wrote and what we said back and forth to each other mattered to them as it mattered to me. Each letter received was always read aloud in front of the whole family. It is just another way a Filipino family monitors, guides, and takes care of its members to the benefit of all the members.

Soon after that letter, the man in the wheelchair sent me a letter with $30 in it. Everybody in my family liked him immediately and said, besides being rich he was the only one I could trust not to hurt me because of his handicapped condition. This might sound harsh to some, but should not be misunderstood. My family's main concern was for my safety and if I was going to insist on writing and meeting a man from another country, they believed they would have less worries if he was severely handicapped. I understood their concern but I had a mind of my own and didn't really want a handicapped man, no matter how safe it might be for me. Every night I prayed and asked God to guide me. I told Him that I was willing to take the handicap gentleman because I knew my family, the older one's advice, was better and more experienced than mine, but I preferred to have a man who could lead and guide me and take care of me instead of me having someone to take care of him. I was willing to do whatever God eventually guided me to do, however, and placed my trust in Him.

The man in the wheelchair eventually wrote me two letters but told me I was too young for him and that he was actually looking for a 30 to 40 year old Filipino woman. He asked that I try and find someone good around that age to write to him. I was glad and relieved at this because he wasn't one of my first choices but I was also disappointed because he was the only one my family felt safely about. I did, for a time, try to find him someone sincere to correspond with but I never did write to him again after those first two letters.

During this time, I was still writing Dale back and forth on nearly a weekly basis. He wrote nice friendly letters and we, my family including my aunts, discussed each and every one as they arrived. I was originally told that a Filipino girl has to write a lot of different men if she is really interested in marrying a foreigner because most of the men will write for a while and then loose interest, deciding a long-distance relationship is too difficult or travel to another country like the Philippines too expensive. "Don't put all of your eggs in one basket," I was often told. So that is why I originally picked out five more names to write. I received responses from four of those five men. The engineer from California kept writing me and telling me he was going to come over to the Philippines to visit me and meet my parents but he never got beyond that point. He told me the same thing in several letters until he finally stopped writing. I and my family thought that was probably best, anyway. By the sound of his letters, we began to believe he was simply looking for a babysitter for his child. I also got a letter from Lonnie, the other North Carolina resident. At the time I didn't know if he and Alan lived close to each other or not. All I knew was that Lonnie lived in the mountains outside Asheville and Alan lived outside Winston-Salem. I liked Alan because

89

he kept sending me little stuffed toys, gifts, and having flowers delivered, making me feel like a movie star. I was the talk of the neighborhood as well as my family and, in the Philippines, a man has to woo a girl's family as well as her in order to succeed. My aunts came by the house every few days to see what I had gotten from Alan. The first time I received flowers everyone was talking about it. It was a big deal in our poor neighborhood to see flowers being delivered to me at our house and then for them to come over and find out they were from an American, all the way from America![2] In fact, the first time flowers were delivered was just before I got off work one day. As I got close to our house I saw a crowd of neighbors gathered around looking in the front door and others standing in the street. I hurried to the house because I became worried something bad had happened to someone in our family. As I arrived, I was greeted by everyone wanting to be the first to tell me an American had sent me flowers! It was an unbelievably proud moment. Mama and I went to church later that evening and prayed to give thanks for my good fortune and for Alan's good health. We wrote back and forth for a while. He was always sending me things. He was a Lutheran but he sent me a nice Rosary one time and tape recordings and pictures.

After Lonnie and I exchanged a couple of letters, Lonnie told me I was too young for him and that he was sorry but this letter would be his last. I was 18 and he was 46, but I was impressed with him because he was so handsome in the photo he had sent me in his first letter and he seemed to know so much about the Philippines and Filipino culture. I liked that he knew so much about my country's history and its people and had cared enough to learn so much about it. Vilma sat down with me and helped me compose a letter to send to him. In it we told him how age did not matter and *why* it did not matter. I guess it was a good letter because after several weeks passed I received another letter from Lonnie and we continued to write back and forth with Vilma helping me write each letter. It took me longer and longer to respond to Dale and Alan's letters and I began to loose interest in them as I wrote Lonnie more and more. My parents were still not too sure about Lonnie. When I got that first picture of him in his initial response to my first letter, he was tanned and handsome with his dark hair neatly combed back but my parents thought he looked like a Filipino movie star named Fernando Po and wondered if Lonnie's look wasn't really just baloney or bogart[3] or perhaps he was arrogant and not to be trusted. Because he had been a policeman, they worried about him, about my safety, and found all kinds of reasons I shouldn't write to him any longer. Of course, my family's decision was to be my decision because of our typical cultural bond and support customs but I continued to argue reasons why I should keep writing to him.

My first photo of Lonnie that resembled
Fernando Po that caused my parents' concern.

Although Vilma was always supportive of me when I wrote letters to Lonnie, my parents and the rest of my family, preferred Alan and the happiness he brought the family upon the delivery of his flowers and other items. When I quite writing to him it made my mother angry. He sent more letters asking me what was wrong, asking me if he had said something upsetting to me, and asking me why I no longer wrote. I was never frank with him about the situation and I still find that embarrassing when I think back about it but in my mind I had chosen Lonnie and I didn't want to argue about it or have to defend my decision with anyone else. I was having enough trouble about it with my family. Although Lonnie was a lot older than me, I thought he was handsome and I liked what he wrote in his letters. Alan was nice too, but he was bald and he was always sending me pictures of himself with his pet cats sitting on his lap. That always bothered me. As I was growing up I was exposed to so many superstitions about cats and their association with witches and warlocks that the mere sight of them still made me uncomfortable.[4]

As I continued to write Lonnie, Mama and all of my aunts kept warning me against him saying "Look at him. Just look at him," as they held his picture. Even though we had policemen in our own family, my mother and my aunts said they could not be trusted. They were womanizers, corrupt and mean. "Just look at him," they would say. "He looks like a strong man. He'll tackle you down when you make him angry."

But Vilma always helped me write my letters to Lonnie, even though she was often tired in the evening, because I would do her chores in order to get her help. On the nights I wanted her to write a letter I would have to wash the supper dishes or whatever she had been assigned to do. She was married by then so she would also sometimes have me clean her house or watch her baby daughter, CherryVell, or do whatever she wanted done. She was smart. She would say, "OK I'll write your letter but you have to do this for me or that for me." It was always a pay-back situation for her letter-writing expertise, so that is why she didn't care who I wrote as long as I worked for it. As time went on, I wrote more and more of the letters to Lonnie. I got out my English dictionary and looked up words I needed, sometimes I found my own words, and sometimes I even copied words and some sentences out of the letters I had gotten from the other pen-pals—I would take their words and give them to Lonnie! The more I did this, the better I got at writing letters in English and the less extra work I had to do for Vilma!

In looking back, I really think it was a miracle—it was fate—that Lonnie and I ever got together. I originally wrote to him even though there was no picture of him in his personal ad—all the others I wrote had displayed pictures with their advertisement—my sister and I were able to convince him to write to me even though I was half his age, nearly everyone in my family was against him, my letter-writing ability was limited but I was able to quickly over-come that, and we developed a close relationship between us even though we were separated by an ocean and a distance of nearly 7,000 miles.

Unlike my other pen-pals, Lonnie's letters were always long—four to six pages or more—and very kind and understanding. I always liked his words. They were usually very thoughtful and sweet. My parents thought he was cheap because he often sent me Philippine stamps that he had purchased to save me postage, but never sent me money, gifts or flowers like some of the others that wrote to me. Of course, what he wrote and talked about was what was most important to me. I would take his letters to work and show them to all my co-workers and they would marvel over each and every one. They would all get excited every time they learned I had received another letter. I was so proud to show them to all my co-workers and they would often ask that I find them an American pen-pal like this one!

CHAPTER 7

Growing up Female

Until just a few years ago, growing up female in the Philippines was of special social significance. Girls were raised from infancy to be feminine and to act feminine and they were made conscious at an early age of the great social honor of being judged by everyone as being beautiful. Every barrio, municipio, city and province had—and still has—its own beauty contests and the most attractive young girls—most often being the daughters of the wealthiest families in the community—were always encouraged to compete. Many others participated in a multitude of religious processions, fiestas, and neighborhood singing and dancing competitions where their beauty was also judged. It was regarded as a great family honor to have a member of its clan selected as a beauty queen. Imelda Marcos, herself, was known for her beauty and in her high school days was called the "Rose of Tacloban," the official beauty title of her town's pageant, and she later went on to become "Miss Manila." Such titles are a big deal in the Philippines and in fact, to this day in the Philippines, any beauty-queen titles ever achieved by a women is always mentioned when introducing her, even if she is past her sixties.

In addition, up through my generation, Filipino girls were instilled with the traditional Asian belief that in public she should always act shy, demure, modest, self-effacing, and be loyal to the end. Most of all, she was taught to never show aggressiveness in public. Behind this facade, or in private and behind the scenes, she was taught to be in charge of the home, in charge of raising the family, and that she was equal to her husband in family affairs, especially in the normal day to day operations and financial transactions of the family.[1]

At the same time, in Filipino culture we were all taught in the old Asian ways that the family was of the upmost importance. From early on, we children were taught that the parents were owed a great debt of gratitude for bringing us into the world. At the same time the parents, themselves, believed they should make any sacrifice necessary for each of their children *because* they brought them into this world. Our obedience to the parents and to the older siblings was taught early in childhood and enforced until adulthood. Moreover, growing up it had become a sense of obligation within each child. The parents, we are taught, are always to be treated with respect and with gratitude throughout our entire lives.[2]

Growing up, a Filipino girl's mother serves as her first role model and teaches her everything she knows about the female's role in society, cultural dynamics, nurturing and taking care of the family, while the older sisters all serve as additional role models and as "deputy mothers," who deserve just as much respect.[3]

Originally, from childhood Filipino girls were taught to take care of their younger siblings, and to play with baby dolls and little dishes. As they got older they were taught to cook and raised in the tradition of respect and devotion to the male. The girls are literally "trained" to be feminine by being taught throughout their lives to be gentle, charming, intelligent, and to dress attractively. Girls in my country have always been raised to be a good wife in the Asian tradition of respect and devotion to her husband. In return for this, all that she expects is that he be honest, sincere, and a responsible and a dedicated husband. To her, his looks and age are not as important as his sincerity and dedication. All of this of course, is not so true today as it was in the past. Even in the Philippines, those that were coming up after me have been more independent and more influenced in Western ways than the girls of my generation.

I can remember when I was young and had just begun to walk, talk, and understand the few words necessary for me to know for my use in daily life, my parents started teaching me all about what a girl's responsibility was in the home. It was important to them that I know my part. They taught me what kind of games I should play, what obligations and chores were mine around the home, and what I should and shouldn't do. One thing I learned was that I shouldn't do any type of boy or man things. There were so many things I learned to do and not to do in those formative years. I think that is one reason why, as I look back now, Mama got so mad at me when I climbed trees. Tree-climbing was actually a boy thing according to their teachings. It was what boys were supposed to do. Not girls. So, whenever she caught me climbing around up in a tree, it made her mad and I got spanked.

As the years passed, throughout my childhood I was taught to do so many things that only girls were supposed to do. I helped prepare some of the food for our meals, I went to school, I babysit my younger brother, and every morning I was responsible for sweeping the floor of our house inside and sweeping the ground or pathways of any trash and debris all around the house on the outside. Once in a while I was responsible for taking lunch to my father and my two brothers to their work at the fish ponds if my mom was too busy with housework or some other chore. In addition, each morning I would help my blind Grandpa get his water at the well, walk him out to the C.R., comb his hair, and all his other morning chores while grandmother picked up and cleaned around her house or was out gathering fuel for the day's cooking needs. During those years, Grandpa would sometimes offer me a peso for my help and sometimes not. Either way, I helped him because Mama had ordered me to do so. But when Grandpa did offer me a peso for my help, I always accepted it because I could use it to buy a snack at school or on my way home afterwards. Once in a while, when no one else was available to accompany him, Grandpa would also use me as his cane for support and his eyes to see when he went into town or any other place he wanted to go. On those trips he would always buy me candy or some treat for my help and I would sit quietly off to one side eating it as he sat and talked with his *barkadas* in town.

I also sang and danced in school and at neighborhood get-togethers as well as volunteered to perform dances and songs in our town fiesta along with my younger brother.

I always had a busy life, including dance
performances in our town's fiestas and at school.

Even with all of this, though, I always believed I was the most hated person in my family. I often believed that I was the bad-luck or the black sheep of the clan. It always seemed Mom had so much stress from me. I couldn't follow her rules without creating problems or do what I was told without back-talk. Girls were not supposed to do such things. Once, out of frustration I guess, Mama even told me that if she had only known about all the problems I would eventually cause her before she had me, she would have buried me before I had ever formed. In fact as I was growing up, whenever she got mad at me, she often referred to the fact that she regretted having me and told me so. I was never sure if she really meant it or just said such things out of anger and frustration. Such comments only came out when I did something wrong or when she was angry at me. I later began to believe that a lot of her anger was the result of papa's affair and that she took it out on me because I was causing her problems about that time. In fact, I think I was acting out more because of that incident too. Even as a kid I understood why she thought I was a problem. I could not stay home long and I had a tendency to wander off and explore. According to her teachings, girls shouldn't do that. I was a curious kid though—I guess—but I was also greatly bored around the house. Sometimes when mom would take a nap around noon I would go off and explore—going to the neighbors to find kids to play with, watch TV with them, or to listen to some of the drama or inspirational radio programs with them. I always tried to come back before Mama would wake up but most of the time I lost control because perhaps the game we were playing had become great fun or because the TV show or soap-opera we were watching had become too interesting to leave. One of my most favorite programs was the American serial "Wonder Women." I just couldn't leave until it had ended. I wanted to identify with her so badly—"Wonder Woman" was my hero and inspiration.

It would make Mama so mad, sometimes. She had no idea where I was when she woke up until I returned home. When my mother had a stroke during my fifth-grade year, I had always believed I was probably the main cause. I was convinced that I had frustrated that poor women so much that I had made her sick and made her hate me. What I wouldn't learn until many years later was that both my sisters, even Vilma, thought *they* were the most hated in the family. Concerned with my own situation, I had never really noticed at the time that Mama treated them the same way, made the same comments, and was just as unhappy about their behavior. Helen even pointed out in later years that I was the only child, besides Richein, who had *not* eventually gone off and lived with other friends or relatives while attending school because of finances or the pressures at home. In fact, whenever the possibility had come up, or had even been suggested, Mama would claim I couldn't move out and live with others because I would only embarrass her—that all I could do was eat and sleep, and I was no good for hard work—apparently ignoring or forgetting all the chores I did around the house and my daily responsibilities with Grandpa!

I remember one incident when one Aunt and Uncle believed Mama and withdrew their offer to have me stay with them. Mama had told them I was a real good eater; that I could eat a lot real fast, but that was about it! At the time, Mama then offered them Helen or Vilma, saying a mother knows her children best and she could defend Helen or Vilma as the best workers in our family but she "should probably just keep Melba at home" with her. So, as Helen later maintained, as things were maybe I *was* "the favorite daughter" after all.

In addition to being taught to play with dolls, doing girl things and having girl chores as I was growing up, the females of past generations through my generation in the Philippines were all taught or raised as teens with how to act and do the women's job as we got older and what was expected of us in adulthood. We were taught that we would always have different chores and different responsibilities than the man. Our main job was to take care of the housework like cooking the food, cleaning the house, washing the clothes and taking care of the smaller brothers and sisters or, once married, the husband and children. That is why my mom and dad were never really concerned if I or my sisters could not finish school because, in Filipino society, the man is supposed to make the money. The woman's job was to take care of the house and the babies and that was learned outside of school. They believed it was good for the women to be educated but that was merely a luxury in our society, not a necessity.

Even as a child, I saw problems with this role. I wanted an education and I wanted to be smart. I wanted to climb trees and to play with any toy that struck my mood. By my teen years I also realized that although I wanted to make the man in my life happy and proud of me, I also wanted a good life and to be treated with respect and be happy myself. I had already seen and heard things that made me believe that foreign men were more trustworthy than Filipino men. I saw many who mistreated their wives every day and remained unemployed, content to sit around in their yard drinking and playing cards with their friends. And as I was growing up I saw sorrows of many kinds caused by the roaming eyes and wandering minds of some of our neighbors and even some of my Aunts and Uncles, married cousins, or some of my our other relatives. What hurt me the most, however, was my father's betrayal. When mom learned of his affair, it seemed that our home began to fall apart. Almost every day there was a fight, or argument, between the two of them. There is no need to go into the details of that betrayal today but it is enough to say that it is an event which I saw much of in my life and in my home that I never wanted to experience in my married life. So, that is when I started to hate men for the way they act and to not trust them for what they say—and not want to believe any of their words. As I grew older I heard gossip and learned that many wives in the Philippines—in our own neighborhood in fact—had been hurt in similar ways by their spouse. So I made the decision to find a man in a foreign land, hoping that they might be better than the men in my own country. With all considerations, I eventually choose the USA as my main interest because of their good record of being loving companions that I had heard about from other women who had married men from there. I also learned that older men were best because there was less chance they would leave me or have wandering eyes. I didn't want the young ones to leave me and hurt me. Some Philippine women had married American servicemen of about their same age and they, too, had experienced problems and had been abandoned or divorced after a few years in the States. I never wanted to be divorced. Never! I had learned that a lot of young men just aren't trustworthy. They flirt, they have roaming eyes and they strut around like a rooster while an older man is usually tired. He has already had enough excitement in his life and simply wants to settle down and have someone he can trust to love and care for him. Usually an older man is more trustworthy.

Of course, all that I really knew about American men was what I had heard or was exposed to as I was growing up. My grandfather had always praised the Americans. I remembered from the time I was tiny he was always telling me stories about them and how important the Americans were to the Philippines during the war, and how brave the American soldiers were, and how he hoped and wished that someday he could move to America and live. But he never did get to realize his dream before he passed away. There have been many times since I have come to America that I have believed that maybe my coming here was the completion of my grandfather's dream. Perhaps he passed his dream on to me and is my guardian angel, looking over my shoulder.

At the same time, I have always worried about my mother's health. She had been admitted to the hospital three times due to her high blood pressure and heart problems. The family slowly paid the various bills for her emergency medical care but just couldn't afford the daily medicines that she needed and we all worried about that. Sometimes I believed I had no choice but to seek help for my family in the only way left that might work out: To find and marry a good foreigner so I could get a job abroad and make enough money to send home. I also wanted to show my mom that I was some-body and that she, and everyone else, was wrong in their judgement and frequent condemnation of me. In the back of my mind I was afraid I might fail and add even more problems for my family to deal with but that didn't stop my ambitions. I had faith and believed that God would guide me in this endeavor. I realized I had been greatly pampered and sheltered throughout my life and that I was weak in nearly all that I did. But I also knew that I loved and pitied my mother and I sincerely worried about her and her health and the assistance that I gave in taking care of her as I was growing up had helped make me strong. It brought me the strength that I needed to go off on an unchartered journey to take care of my entire family.

Such beliefs and reasoning might sound too contrived and calculating for some people. I am sure criticism of this is easy but many Filipinas and other women from Third World and East European countries try to control their destiny by this method.[4]

Love can come in many different ways. Even though today there have been many couples who have met and married through match-making services throughout America, there are still a lot of people who criticize such proceedings. These same people fail to notice that nearly fifty-percent of the so-called "accepted" marriages in the United States end in divorce even though these same couples knew each other for long periods of time and in some cases even grew up together or attended high school or college together.

Then too, for many Filipino women, the age of the man doesn't matter as much as his stability—both financially and emotionally. To our way of thinking, the older men are considered better off financially and less likely to commit adultery. What matters most is the love and respect he gives to his wife and his treatment of her. That's why many of my relatives wanted me to marry the man in the wheelchair. Not only was he generous but he couldn't easily commit adultery and they believed I could outrun him if he tried to mistreat me.

Another great influence on my life and on my decision was my Uncle Dictivo. Ever since I was a little girl he had always traveled abroad. Uncle Dictivo works as a Chief Engineer on a cargo ship and often goes out to sea on contract for several months or sometimes even a year at a time. When he returns home to his family he always brings all kinds of exotic gifts such as Hershey chocolates and a wide variety other candies, various foods, and presents. Although he was gone a lot, his family always seemed well off. As a little girl I was always envious of his children, my cousins, because they always seemed to have an abundance of nearly everything. But Uncle Dictivo was always very generous. He would also bring gifts to the rest of the family—his brothers and sisters, to share with their families. Sometimes he would give Mama expensive soaps, towels, or T-shirts from far-off lands, and others in the family would receive watches, jackets, and similar items. As I grew older, I began to dream that I too would someday go to far off exotic lands and bring or send back gifts to my family to bring smiles and tears of happiness to all their faces.

CHAPTER 8

Marriage

Grandpa Floro Tumulak passed away on December 26, 1993. It was a very sad time in my life. I loved him very much. He had always seemed to be on my side most of the time and he was always giving me candy or money for candies. When I was a little girl that had always seemed so important to me. And he was always supportive of me in other ways. Although he had often teased his own daughter Aling about her looks, he was very protective of me. Many in my family made fun of me for being short—calling me midget or monkey—or teased me about my flat nose by telling me to quit breathing whenever a breeze blew out a nearby candle or oil lamp but Lolo Floro would defend me and make them stop. In addition, because I was short and dark-skinned, I had always thought my cousin Celia was much prettier than me because she was tall and light skinned. But Grandpa always called her "*put-put-put*" because when she was a tiny little girl at family gatherings they would all get her to start dancing and eventually she would get so excited dancing she would begin to *put-put-put*, or let off loud gas, in her pants and they would all laugh. Grandpa always told me that I was a lot prettier than "*put-put-put*."[1]

While I acted as his guide or caretaker he would tell me so many stories about America and the Americans. He had so many different stories about the war and what he had learned from the American soldiers that he had fought along side. He greatly respected all of them. There is no doubt in my mind Lolo Floro's attitude and beliefs was partly responsible for me becoming so interested in America and wishing to marry an American man as I grew up. Many times before he died, Grandpa Floro had told me how he wished that he could go to America and live among his old Army friends. He told me about how kind all of the American people were and about how grateful he was for what they did for us—all the Filipino people—in World War II. He always said that the American people were the best people he had ever met and, whether black or white, they were all nice. I guess when you are fighting side by side for your lives, depending on each other for survival, you form some very deep bonds.

As I look back, I realize Grandpa Floro must have had many close American friends during the war.

So it was perhaps with this in mind that I began to write Americans and eventually narrowed my interests down to one American man who, although he wasn't a soldier, was a policeman in a big city or—as Lonnie often claimed: an "urban soldier."

We wrote many letters back and forth for nearly a year and began calling each other on the telephone to talk. At the time, my family had no phone in our house so Vilma, or sometimes Helen, would take me to the local Philippines Long Distance Telephone Company (PLDT) in Lapu-Lapu City where we would place a "collect call" to Lonnie on one of the public pay phones at the front of the building. We would usually call sometime around 1:00, 2:00 or 3:00 in the afternoon but I was often disappointed with his response when he answered the telephone. Lonnie never seemed very happy to hear from me until we had talked for a little while. I begin to think maybe he was losing interest in me or didn't want us calling him "collect." Finally my sister and I learned that when we called him at 1, 2 or 3 P.M. Philippine time, it was actually 1, 2 or 3 A.M. where Lonnie lived. He had been reluctant to tell us that it was the middle of the night where he was and wasn't sure if we knew it or not but he didn't want to discourage us from calling. Eventually Vilma and I began calling Lonnie at 6:00 or 7:00 in the evening so that we could catch him early in the morning as he was getting ready for work. We did this for nearly six more months in addition to writing two or three letters a week.

Eventually, Lonnie came to the Philippines to visit me and my family. A few months before he arrived, however, there had been talk in my neighborhood that some foreigner had been going around asking neighbors and relatives about me while I was at work. I was told that the foreigner, riding a motorcycle, had been asking all kinds of questions but everyone had acted like they either didn't know me or had refused to answer his questions to protect me because they didn't know who he was and had trouble understanding his accent or slag anyway. We were all sad and somewhat disappointed over this because we all believed that one of my pen-pals, perhaps Lonnie, had sent someone to check on my background or trustworthiness. We never did find out who the stranger was or who had sent him.[2]

When Lonnie did get to the Philippines, I wasn't so impressed upon our first meeting. As he came into the terminal within view, he looked tired and haggard and his hair was messed up. I even remember thinking to myself, "Where is this handsome man I saw in those pictures?" He did seem nice though. It wasn't until he got to our house, shaved and cleaned up that I realized how mistaken I had been. He was very handsome and his original look, I later realized, was a result of his long plane trip—although he admitted he had tried to shave and clean up in the Manila airport restroom but found it was entirely too crowded and had eventually ran out of time before his flight left for Mactan.

At first I thought he was hard-of-hearing. My family and I spoke "perfect" English but there was so much Lonnie didn't understand or needed repeated. Vilma, Richein and I were quite fluent, in fact, while Helen, my older brothers and my parents were limited in their English from lack of use over the years. I later learned that Lonnie could hear fine. He just had trouble understanding our accent as we spoke. I hadn't realized there was a difference. I had always thought English was English.

When all of my co-workers learned that Lonnie had come to the Philippines they all came over to our house as a group to visit one day. I was proud because they were all impressed with his looks and told me so, but each time I left the room that day I had my brother Richein sit with Lonnie, afraid one of my friends might try to steal him away! I even worried about one of my Aunts and a cousin who kept coming around our house wanting to see and talk with Lonnie and had either my mom or Richein stay with them whenever I had to leave the room for any reason.

Many Philippine girls believe that ALL American men have a very big *otin*—or penis—anyway, much larger than those of any Asian men. One day while I was still working, one of these co-workers had brought a huge over-sized rubber penis to work and caused much laughter in our department when she showed it to me and asked "Melba, are you sure you can you handle this" and because of my small size and innocence said "Melba, this will kill you!" They all got a big laugh about it but I was embarrassed and secretly worried about what she said for sometime afterwards.

One day Lonnie went in and talked with my father privately, seeking his permission to ask me to marry him. After a good conversation Papa gave him permission, requesting a church wedding, and was quite proud when Lonnie proposed to me later that day. Of course, I said "yes."

It wasn't an easy decision for either one of us. I had to consider my future, moving away from my family—I had never been away from them for any length of time—and moving to a country that I only knew about from books, magazines, movies and TV, with an older foreigner that I only knew from letters, telephone conversations, and the short times that we had spent together. Lonnie would have similar concerns about me and my ability to live in another country. In addition, in order to be married in a Catholic church, Lonnie had to be Catholic but he had been raised Methodist. Knowing how important having a big wedding in a Catholic church was for me and my family, however, he was interested in converting to Catholicism. We went into Cebu City to talk with the local priest who referred us to the Bishop of the Diocese of Cebu. After a long conversation, Bishop Adelito Abella told us that he would be interested in marrying us personally if Lonnie would agree to attend daily classes over the following three weeks and convert to Catholicism. Lonnie agreed and each morning for three weeks he went by trike and cab to Cebu City and attended the classes. At the conclusion, he was baptized by Bishop Abella, an event attended by me, friends, and all of my immediate family, and then we all went out had a celebration afterwards.

At another meeting with the Bishop and his staff we made arrangements to be married at the ornate three-hundred year old Cebu Metropolitan Cathedral at Legaspi and Mabini Streets in downtown Cebu City. We had originally hoped for a Valentine's Day wedding but that date had already been fully scheduled so we chose February 18.

The main entrance to historic Cebu Metropolitan Cathedral,
built by the Spanish in 1786

One evening while we were alone and talking about the future, Lonnie informed me that he was unable to have children because he had a vasectomy after the third child of his first marriage. He said he had planned to have the procedure reversed without me knowing it before we were married but then found out it would cost anywhere from five to six thousand dollars or more. He said he couldn't afford it now but perhaps in the future. I was angry! This was something he should have told me about before now. This was something he should have told me about before we had ever met face to face! It would have been much easier for me to give him up back then. I didn't even know what a vasectomy was but I knew he meant we couldn't have babies like we had talked about.

I told him I didn't want to get married. He tried to talk to me but I just sat there and said nothing. I couldn't even look at him. I just sat there and stared at the wall of my room in deep thought and ignored everything he was saying.

Finally he gave up trying to talk to me. He quietly got up and went into the other room where my parents were and told my papa that I no longer wanted to get married and that the wedding should be called off.

Startled with disbelief Papa, getting up, responded with, "Whaat?" as he came into my room and stood in the doorway looking at me. "Oh she's just joking," he finally said as he watched me for a moment. "She can joke very good with a straight face."

I sat there without a word for some time, continuing to think about the situation as Papa tried to talk to me. Mama came around the corner looking at me without a word. I saw tears rolling down from her eyes. Lonnie should have told me before, I kept thinking to myself. He wasn't being honest. He wasn't being fair. Should I tell them? I wasn't sure. I wasn't even sure what *I wanted to do* yet.

But I was sure that I did love him. He was kind and gentle. He was very caring and seemed so protective and loving of me. I had chosen him over the other men even when mama and some of her friends had tried to convince me to consider others. Now she and Papa thought he was the greatest and loved him as well. "Perhaps this was fate," I thought to myself. Perhaps God intended for me to choose Lonnie over the others and not have children. Maybe God had other plans.

Finally I admitted to Papa I was just joking and I heard him and Mama give out a sigh of relief. I hadn't realized my decision had become so important to them in such a short time! I never did reveal to them the reason for my anger that day.

Later, Lonnie and I talked about it more as he apologized again for lying or misleading me about having children. He felt guilty about having mislead me and I didn't feel sorry for him in the least bit—and told him so.

When Lonnie first arrived in my country, Grandma Tumulak, in addition to having Alzheimer's disease, had suffered several strokes and was confined to her bed to live out her last days. Uncle Tonyo and Aunt Lena took over the responsibility of her daily care and lived in her house, next door to my parents, with her. I proudly took Lonnie over so they could meet. I introduced him to her but she was unable to respond. However, she did lay there looking at him, following his movements with her eyes. Lonnie tried to talk with her briefly but I knew her English was poor and she probably didn't understand much that he said. Poor Grandma, all she could do was lay there on her mat in the front room and watch us and listen to us.[3]

In the Philippines, upon applying for a marriage license at the local city hall the prospective couple is then scheduled for a counseling session with a marriage counselor. The couple is also required to separately answer a ten-page questionnaire that covers a whole range of their individual attitudes on marriage including their attitudes on relationships in general, love, relatives, in-laws, family, money, finances, and sex. These forms are then sealed in an envelope to be turned in to the counselor for review in preparation for the up-coming session.

My husband was quite impressed with this procedure and after the session told me that he thought it was all conducted very intelligently and professionally. We met with a Ermelita C. Degamo at the City Social Welfare and Development Office in the Lapu-Lapu City and had about a one hour interview and discussion about marriage and all of the other related subjects. Lonnie and I both thought the counselor was a highly educated and intelligent interviewer. She, afterward, told us that she thought we had a good healthy attitude about marriage and wished us the best of luck.

By the time my parents and I and Lonnie began planning my wedding in greater detail, my aunts, my sisters and several family friends had also became involved in the process. A family friend living in the Beverly Hills section of Cebu City wanted to host a catered reception of her own. This we agreed to and she then asked Lonnie to help out financially. This surprised him but he agreed to it. Before long we were planning out a gigantic wedding at the Cebu Metropolitan Cathedral followed by a catered dinner-party reception with a large three-tiered wedding cake in Cebu City to be attended by several hundred people, including all of my extended family and friends, and another dinner reception at my parents' house soon afterwards to be attended by all of my relatives along with all of our neighbors and friends. At this reception we would slaughter a calf, a goat, have chickens on a rotisserie, plenty of fish, and roasted pig. Papa, helped by several of my uncles and brothers, was in charge of preparing this feast.

Lonnie later said that the whole affair seemed highly disorganized with a lot of spur-of-the-moment planning in comparison to similar American affairs and lacked any sense of detailed advance planning, which seemed to put everything in a constant state of confusion. Yet, he was surprised and proud how we brought it all together in time.

On the morning of our wedding everyone was up by dawn preparing for the day. Papa and the others had worked throughout the night preparing the day's wedding feast, slaughtering and cleaning all the animals and gathering up all the fresh fish, spices, vegetables, and fruits at the market. A number of local beauticians arrived at our house and began doing all the women's hair and applying makeup for a truly professional look. Photographers and video crews arrived and began recording the event while others arrived throughout the morning bringing flowers and more food.

Finally, the time arrived and we were driven to the church in separate vehicles. Several people, including my mother, were upset. The car that was supposed to drive me to the church, with flowers splayed out all over its hood, took Lonnie when he arrived at the front of our house. I was taken to the church soon afterwards in another car having less flowers. Meanwhile Aunt Siding, one of our ten chosen God Mothers invited to the wedding, became upset and went back home. She had missed her assigned car because they had ran out of room—it had became a first come, first served situation—and she felt ignored. Her feelings hurt, she walked home to ignore the wedding.

In my country, the bride and groom and their parents are responsible for providing transportation to the church for all of their guests invited to attend the wedding. It was especially important in this situation because the church in Cebu City was several miles away. Because we are not highly professional in organizing such an affair, the whole situation and the people involved often fall into complete chaos and it soon becomes an "every one for themselves" situation! Before long everyone was scurrying everywhere with no organization at all. Like Lonnie later said, it was like organized chaos that soon lost its organization.

I was amazed that he had observed this because, at the time, he seemed oblivious to the whole situation. I guess, like a duck, he was able to remain calm on the surface. I, on the other hand, was beginning to think someone was actually trying to obstruct my wedding or bring it to a halt. I didn't have time to be frustrated over it . . . but my Mama sure did!

The dress I wore was a very ornate and delicate flowing gown designed by my relatives and handmade by my Ante Solara. As my Papa and I came down the carpeted aisle my Mama became somewhat irritated that my fluffy dress was causing me some problems as I walked along. Parts of the flowing skirt continued to get tangled in my feet and I smiled widely in embarrassment. A long wedding procession proceeded down the isle before me that consisted of my cousin Roselyn, who was my Maid of Honor, and five bridesmaids, three little flower girls and two little boy ring and Bible bearers. Lonnie, my brother Ferdinand who was his Best Man, and five groomsmen waited at the alter with Bishop Abella.

Me, at my wedding. I felt like a fairy-tale princess.

The Bride, the Groom, and our Wedding Party.

The wedding went well and we both repeated our nuptials perfectly but when Lonnie started to place the ring on my finger as directed, he took a hold of my left hand and the Bishop whispered in panic, "No, no! Right hand! Place it on her right hand!" Without a word, Lonnie quickly followed his directions even though, as an American, it was probably confusing.

Lonnie would later learn that the practice of wearing the wedding rings on the left hand is purely rooted in an Olde English superstition that there is a vain running from the left hand directly to the heart. Roman Catholics have traditionally worn them on the ring finger of the right hand based upon the Bible. Scripturally it has always been the practice to wear important rings on the right hand because it was the hand of authority and power and completes the pledge of commitment. The "power and authority," of course, comes from the right hand of God. Thus, Catholics of many European countries wear the wedding ring on the right hand and that is how it was practiced and eventually introduced to the Filipinos by the Spaniards.

Following our two big dinner receptions, Lonnie, me, my brothers, my sisters and their husbands, and my Mama and Papa all played music tapes and danced together and laughed and talked and celebrated until late at night. The following morning we all got up and they bid us good-bye as friends took Lonnie and me to the Shangri-La International Resort on the other end of Mactan Island for our week-long Honeymoon.

The Shangri-La was the most beautiful place that I think I had ever been. I had heard much about it but I had never been there. Only hotel guests are allowed beyond its guarded front gates so the most that any of us island Filipinos have seen from the street is the immaculate white hotel building off in the distance and the beautiful flowering trees, shrubs and plants within sight throughout the property. The resort with its richly ornate interior, plentiful and beautifully laid out food buffets, its clean private beach, and multiple swimming pools—one having a long slide and waterfall—made me think that I was living in paradise. I thought this must be how all Americans live. It was great. I was going to really enjoy this life! The great food buffets with the "all you can eat" breakfasts, lunches and dinners was beyond my belief. It was the first time I had ever eaten at a buffet set up like this and Lonnie had to help me or explain the proper procedures on several occasions. The first time I filled my plate to over-flowing and part of it fell off on my way to our table. I had been afraid they would take the food away before I had gotten my fill. I was embarrassed when I dropped some of the food items off my plate and various staff rushed out from all directions to help me to the table and to clean up the floor! While we were there, I even saw the Filipino movie star Mickie Cojuanco several times in the lobby and, on one afternoon, she was even in the pool with Lonnie and me.

To Lonnie's amazement, each day a member of my family would come over to the resort to see me. The second day we were there my parents came by and brought as some homemade food that was left over from our wedding feast. Supposedly they didn't realize the hotel had every kind of food imaginable. They said they were afraid we would get hungry, especially after our first night. Lonnie thought that was funny. The third day, my brother Carlito, came by to visit and on the fourth day, my sister Helen. Each time, the guards at the front gate would stop them and call or contact us—we were down at the pool the day Helen came—to make sure these "strangers" were someone we knew and that it was OK to let them in to see us. Lonnie couldn't believe that in such a short period of time they had all began to miss me so much but by the second visit he then realized that their real intent was to check on me and my welfare. By then he thought it was humorous and began to expect and look forward to their daily visits and even predict which family member might come. On the fifth day, when we planned to leave the resort, my father came by with transportation for us and we had him wait and accompany us back home.

Lonnie and I stayed with my family for a couple more days, visiting and taking walks through the neighborhood, until it was time for Lonnie to return to the USA. We knew I wouldn't be allowed to go with him to the United States until Lonnie had returned and filed out all the papers and submitted all of the proper forms and documents for a visa—a process that would require me to be interviewed at the American Embassy in Manila and undergo medical exams and other procedures that might take several months to complete.

On the day of his departure, all of my family accompanied us to the airport for several hours of tearful goodbyes. This was a terribly sad day for all of us. Way back in the back of my mind, I was afraid that he might return to America and forget all about me.

Trying to convince a man to marry you by long distance is a very sad story to tell. But, I guess, you're gonna do what you're gonna do. Many women write to a foreign man for several months and then go to their pen-pal's country to visit on a Fiancé Visa. Being on a Fiancé Visa does not leave a lot of options from which to choose. The visitor has certain limitations set out by the government in order to stay in that country. In the USA a lady has a certain length of time to marry their acquaintance when they arrive on a Fiancé Visa, otherwise they must return to their home country. If they meet their pen-pal and they both like and respect each other, everything works out fine. But if the guy turns out to be mean, abusive, a criminal or somehow dishonest or takes advantage of the women, then her life can become even more difficult and sad. She has to decide if she will go ahead and marry her fiancé—even if it's against her better judgement—just to stay in America and keep her family name clean in the eyes of those back in her country or to return to her home unmarried. Of course, returning often makes the women an embarrassment to her family and a laughing-stock in the eyes her neighbors and friends who knew why she had left. Of coarse, on the other hand, she can always stay in the foreign land in a bad marriage to a terrible man in order to have a better opportunity and, perhaps, make a better life for herself. Unfortunately, some women find themselves in just such a situation and do eventually decide they "might as well give it a shot" and "who knows?"—just hope for the best.

At the Shangri-La International Resort on Mactan Island.

Sometimes, though, we also read about their death and think about how sad her life must have been or how badly she must have hoped for a better life to take such a chance.

By the Grace of God—and the insistence of my parents—I, on the other hand, went about it differently. I had no intentions of going to America on such a visa. Even though it might take longer to get to the USA, it was important to me to have a wedding in the Catholic church in the Philippines where my parents and all of my family could attend and enjoy. The resulting Spouse or Immigrant Visa that would be obtained afterwards would be a long wait but safer. Like the Fiance Visa, however, it also has additional disadvantages. True, I had the advantage that most women want—being wed where my whole family could attend and to have the honor and respect of the watchful eyes of the community. And the most important: To make my parents very proud. But I was not thinking—nor even aware of—what the American public thought of the situation or what many in this country would say about my marriage or how I met my husband and grew to love him dearly. Not until I came to this country and found out that many people have many things to say. I thought everything was OK, but in fact, it was sometimes worse than I ever imagined. But many women in my own country also found much to criticize about it. Either out of jealously or envy they would criticize my decision or try and put bad thoughts or worries in my head.

Meeting a man like this, of course, you likely gamble yourself hoping for the best. I waited for almost a year to be united with my husband and during that long period of waiting my friends and neighbors did all that they could to create doubt, fear, and other gigantic monstrous thoughts in my head. Which, of coarse, was helped along by rumors and gossip from other friends, relatives, and people I met as time passed.

Being married is supposed to be a safe and secure feeling right? Well not for me. Honestly, I was terrified from the day that my husband had left me behind when he went back to America. I shouldn't feel that way, but I did. Especially when I called him long-distance every week and he sounded tired or had no excitement to talk to me on that particular day I felt like he was hiding something and my friends assured me that I was probably right. I did not know, at that time, that he was so tired because I was still calling him early in the morning, like at 2:00 a.m. which was 2:00 in the afternoon Philippine time and I didn't know then that he was filing all kinds of papers and contacting his local Congressman and Senator trying to rush the paperwork to get me to America sooner. Still, I always had lots of doubt in my mind. I guess part of the reason was because of my father's betrayal—that one incident so saddened me that it was always in my thoughts when issues of trust came to my mind.

I worried that Lonnie was going to forget me or maybe get tired of our long separation or of all the paperwork he had to file and the money he had to send in to the government with each of the forms he was required to file and that he might just decide to leave me at my parents' home forever. I couldn't do anything but speculate as I listened to the comments and implications made by my friends, some of my relatives and some of my acquaintances. Whenever they would see me they would ask when I thought I was going to America or why hadn't my husband returned and gotten me yet. I, of course, would always have to answer that I did not know or that it took a long time and then they would just fake their understanding and act like I had been taken advantage of as they walked away.

The fact is, it *has* happened to some Filipino women that their husbands—after a wedding ceremony and an enjoyable honeymoon—went back home to their country and were gone forever or found another women during that long wait to get them, so it is possible. I worried, "What if this will happen to me?" It would disgrace my family and I would become a big failure to them and a big laugh to all. And what about my dream of being different and having a good life away from poverty. "Is it going to fail? If it is, then I will return to my cloudy life and I bet it will be worse than before. Then I *will* wish I was never born."

But then my positive side of my brain would become dominate and bring me comfort and tell me not to worry because Lonnie was trustworthy. "Why would he come such a long way to waste his time and money, not to mention the danger he faced coming to a strange land he had never been to," I would think to myself, "and in addition he was still contacting me by letter every week and I still talked to him twice or sometimes three times a week on the phone and he was sending me money for me and my family." So, I got a good fighting spirit in me and ignored the comments made by others—knowing that someday I would have the last laugh—and of course my faith in God always remained and supported me all the way, until my nightmare of waiting was over.

Thank goodness nothing like that ever happened to me. My husband didn't abandon me. After all, no man in my country would ever want me anymore once something like that happened because, in the Philippines being a virgin is still of the up-most importance to all the men. I'm not a virgin anymore after our honeymoon so no man would consider me except, perhaps out of pity or just to use me for their needs. Such things is what I feared.

After the wedding and Lonnie went back to the America, I received a letter from Cebu Micro Electronics, where I worked, asking for an explanation of my month-long absence. I had used up my two weeks vacation and had taken two more for my wedding, my honeymoon and to be with Lonnie until he was to return to the USA. I hadn't officially quit because I had no idea if Lonnie would really show up for our wedding or if he might get cold feet and chicken out and leave me stranded without a husband and without a job.

Then my life would become even more pitiful. So just in case, and to cover all my bases, I never told them I wanted to quit and I never told Lonnie my two weeks vacation had ended and I needed to go back to work. The letter informed me that I was a valued employee and they wanted me to return and explain my absence. Upon receiving this letter I realized that I had a slim hope or fifty-fifty chance to continue with a good job until I joined my husband in America. I studied the letter and made a final decision to return and take my chances that they really wanted me back. I had no idea when or how long I had to wait to be united with Lonnie and my family depended on me for financial help. I decided to go explain my situation to my bosses and ask for their forgiveness for my unexplained disappearance. Actually I knew that even with this letter I could be terminated for not showing up during the extra two weeks that I had taken. Being sorry was no guarantee I would get my job back but I decided it was worth a try. Perhaps they just wanted to tell me to my face that I was fired for my decision but I decided to take the chance, and again, "who knows?"

I went to the company and brought the letter with me. I talked to a lady in the personnel department—who seemed very nice—and explained what had happened in my life during the past four weeks, about spending time at the Shangri-La resort, and why I made the decision that I had about spending as much time with my husband as possible. The lady was very understanding, explained that I had apparently been a good employee previously and that, perhaps, I could continue working there until I left for America. In fact, she did go to the trouble to help me get my previous position back—my previous position of Quality Control Inspector—for which I remain thankful to her forever. In fairness to myself, though, I also had earned it. I had been one of their most dedicated and hard working employees and that too was why they had accepted me back—for which I was still very grateful and thought it was another favor from God. In addition, the company was very smart too. They knew that even though I was gone for two weeks on vacation that they would have to include on my next pay check, I was gone two more weeks that they would not have to pay for and they could still save even more money if they kept me rather than hiring a replacement to train and have additional expenses to cover for a new employee.

Finally, after nearly eleven months I received a letter from the U.S. Embassy in Manila informing me that I had been scheduled for an interview for consideration of a Visa to America. Examining the letter closer, my sister and I discovered that it had arrived exactly one week *after* my scheduled interview date!

Devastated over this, I cried hysterically throughout the day. "How could they do this?" "What was I to do now?" I couldn't believe it.

My sister and I decided to go call Lonnie and find out what I should do. When we got to the telephone company at Lapu-Lapu and called, he too became upset and said he would call the embassy and his political representatives to complain and find out what to do and to call him later in the week to get further instructions.

I later learned that North Carolina's Senator Jesse Helm's office contacted the U.S. Embassy in Manila and straightened out the matter, The embassy, in turn, contacted me and made apologies. When we called Lonnie a few days later, he told us to contact the embassy and make a new appointment for a time most convenient for me and my family. We did and then made arrangements for a family friend, Johnny Pepito whose sister had married an American and lived in the state of Virginia, to escort us to and around Manila. My parents and I had never been on an airplane and had never been to Manila.

On October 3, 1997, I and my parents and Johnny Pepito boarded Philippine Airline flight #835 for Manila at 5:30 A.M. I was so scared and afraid to get on the airplane but I knew it was something that had to be done. My Mama and Papa were just as scared and nervously joked about it. When we arrived at the Mactan International Airport, I was amazed at the number of people I saw from all the different places—from all around the world—many dressed so differently in so many different styles. I, nor my parents, had ever had the experience of going to different places outside of Cebu Province, except to nearby Leyte. We were fortunate to have our guide, Johnny, because we had never been to our capital city and did not know where or how to get to the U.S. embassy. Lonnie had sent us enough money to cover the airplane tickets, food and other expenses for the day for all of us, including our tourist guide. We were very thankful for that.

It was an uneventful one hour plane flight to Manila. After we landed we went directly to the embassy. As we entered the gated area a security guard stopped us and I showed him my letter and explained about the new appointment for my interview and F.B.I. fingerprints. He informed us that I had to proceed on my own inside while my companions stayed outside the gated area. This made me nervous. I had to proceed on my own without my family's support and help beyond this point. He handed me a form to fill out and afterwards directed me to a cashier to pay for the fingerprinting procedure. Meanwhile, I wondered why there was so many people sitting around inside and standing in various long lines all around the embassy. There were Filipinos standing all around waiting for interviews, fingerprinting, and for various other formalities. I soon found myself among them. By 10:30 we were done. I was happy and relieved to have it over.

We all went and had lunch and then Johnny took us to Nayon Filipino, a nearby park that had scaled-down replicas and exhibits of all of the tourist attractions found throughout the Philippine Islands.

Our first time, ever, in Manila. L-R: Mama, me and Papa.

After we returned home, I continued to work the rotating shifts at Cebu Electronics. Nearly 12 weeks passed before I heard from the embassy again. I received a letter notifying me they had scheduled an appointment for me at the end of January, 1998, to return for my physical exam, another interview, and all the final procedures for my Visa to America.

Very happy and pleased, I contacted Lonnie and advised him of the appointment. He asked if I wanted him to proceed over to accompany me—which we had previously discussed as a possibility—and I asked that he would.

Lonnie returned to the Philippines on January 21 and stayed a few days with me and my family before our scheduled appointment in Manila. He and I then flew into the capital city on January 25, the day before the appointment, and stayed overnight at the Manila Holiday Inn, within six blocks of the American Embassy. The following morning we got up early, had a big breakfast at the hotel, and then walked down to the embassy, situated in front of Manila Bay—where Lonnie pointed out that the U.S. naval forces under Admiral Dewey fought the Spanish in 1898, separating the Philippines from Spain and placing our country under U.S. administration until World War II broke out—and got into a long line that stretched beyond the building. We eventually got the attention of a security guard, showed him our letter of appointment, and was allowed to stand in line inside the building. Later we were escorted into an office where we were interviewed about our marriage, turned over all of our forms and papers, allowed the authorities to review our private letters and correspondence that Lonnie and I had exchanged over the past couple years, review our wedding pictures, affidavits, licenses and forms before I was finally issued a Visa allowing me to accompany my husband to the United States. As a final requirement, I underwent a battery of medical tests, x-rays, questions and more forms afterwards before the issuance of the approval papers.

We were both very happy and excited as a result and glad to have it all over. Since our return flight wasn't scheduled until late that night, we spent the rest of the day site-seeing around Manila. After walking along and looking at Manila Bay again and going inside the historic Manila Hotel on the north end of the Bay, we went to lunch at a Wendy's restaurant where Lonnie introduced me to the taste of a frosty—a chocolate ice cream treat. While we were there, two little Filipino street children watched us through the plate glass window as we ate. As we left, Lonnie purchased a couple of cheese burgers and gave them to the little poor boys as we came out of the restaurant. I thought that was really nice and sweet of him and it made the two little boys so happy and excited. They thanked him over and over as they took the burgers and went to the side of the building to eat. We then walked around an artist district near Manila's Central Market that had numerous paintings on display and for sale and went into a number of Book Shops so Lonnie could search for a few used books on Philippine history. Then we walked through Rizal Park and looked at the flower displays and the ornate water fountains, saw the Memorial and the site of Jose Rizal's execution and watched the changing of the guards, visited a little post office selling stamps to collectors, of which Lonnie had an interest, and then we walked over and toured the National Museum. Tired out, we rested for a while in another park before getting something to eat for supper and then getting a taxi to head for the airport.

We spent another week with my family before we left for America. That day all the members of my family, including my brothers and sisters and all of their children and spouses, as well as Jun and Bining Potot, dear friends of our family and two of our sponsors at our wedding, accompanied us to the airport to see us off. The Potots stopped at a Goldilocks Bakery on the way there and bought us a big box of bakery goods to take with us on the airplane to snack on.

As anticipation for my new future grew, it was becoming more and more exciting and more and more scary.

CHAPTER 9

America Bound

I have always had great respect for any Filipina who will sacrifice her own well-being and leave her country to work and live among strangers in order to provide a better life for herself and her family. In the Philippines we call such women *bayanis*—heros. No matter what some people might think in other countries, to me—to most Filipinos—such people are regarded as great adventurers—brave people who are willing to take a chance to benefit their families as well as themselves. Every one of them, like me, has a different story. Some of their stories are sad and some of their stories are good or inspiring but we all have similarities in our aim—in our goals in life. Our goal is to help our family out, get out of poverty or the "third world," and to have a better life for ourselves. Yes, some of us come to this country in the nice way or in a highly respected way such as the nurses, doctors, or engineers while some people—like me—arrive in America by marriage and are sometimes criticized or made fun of a little bit, but it is OK. I'd like to be able to explain the various reasons for my decisions just to make people understand my point of view but I have learned that no one can fit in my shoes but me. I have also learned that most people in this country don't care to hear the stories or the reasons for our decisions from people like me. They have already made their mind up about us and that's OK too. I understand.

What *really* matters is that I am happy and that I make my husband and my family happy. Other people will always have critical comments about anyone's decision about anything.

Another problem often faced by people like me is the mistaken belief that we Asian or Filipino wives are submissive to our husbands. I have heard many times that the American men love to marry a Filipino woman because we are known to be a submissive wife. Filipino women are believed to do whatever their husband's please but it's not true at all. I can say "No" if I don't like to do something and so can he. Like any other women, we Filipinas have our limits and we can agree or disagree on anything. We allow ourselves to make such decisions like any other women. If we don't like something we say "no." We do not enter a marriage that is all for him or all for me. We have to give and take like anything else. It is not "take it all." We have discussions with our husbands like all wives should about the various everyday decisions. True, we have been brought up and taught not to argue with our spouse in public or to throw a fit about some decision in front of other people—but we make ourselves understood and our ideas known in the privacy of our own home or in a constructive way in family or husband and wife decisions. Every now and then people ask me and other Filipino wives such silly questions and some are very offensive. They ask, only half kidding, if we were drunk when we married the older men, or ask if he is rich and did we marry for money or because he had a big *otin*. There are times I wish I could explain things better so they could understand. I just can not find a good answer or put into words what would provide them a good understanding or a satisfactory answer. But then I realize it would be a waste of time. Even if I could provide all kinds of intelligent explanations, such people will still have their own opinions or beliefs. Besides, there is a saying that you cannot imagine what a person's life is like until you walk in their shoes. So such people can guess about it all they want and they can form their own opinions based on their own perverted beliefs or misunderstandings but they will never see the true colors of what a person's life is like until they wear that other person's shoes—or go through the same experiences that other person endured in their life.

Also, I have since learned that, like in the Philippines, there are many Filipino women who are being treated wrongly by their spouses right here in America. Usually its because of the differences in their cultures, how they were brought up, or just a general lack of trust in each other. Of coarse lots of gossip and some confusion among the Filipino women makes it difficult for a lot of couples to get along well and sometimes such misunderstandings make it really hard for some of these couples to handle the married life. The couple who is both willing to understand each other and who are willing to sacrifice their differences are more likely to have a nicer life. If they are both willing to give and take—not just her pushing him or him pushing her to do things that she or he don't want to do—these couples are more likely to have a harmonious life. And most important of all is to have God as their guide and counselor as they journey through their married life. Having all of this knowledge and understanding, however, Lonnie and I have still endured some rocky beginnings. Sometimes we had to argue until we learned to understand each other's beliefs and needs.

In my case, my life has changed dramatically since I was a little girl. I have become much more independent and sure of myself. I make my opinion known about any family discussions—both with Lonnie and with my parents—and I insist on taking part in all financial decisions. The older I get, the bolder I have become. I have learned to face things that used to break my heart and to handle situations that used to scare me.

My favorite portrait of my husband and me.

I loved and respected Lonnie based on what I had learned about him through all of our letters, phone calls and the time we had spent together but I also realized I wouldn't *really* know him until we had lived together for a few years. I was hoping to have a good future and was looking for something different in life. A life different than what my parents had ever had. But my attitude *Bahala na*—come what may—or *Que Sera Sera*—whatever will be, will be—best served me as I prepared for my new life in America.

I had heard many different stories about Filipinas who had married foreigners. Some accounts were good and some were bad. But many sounded like they had acquired a good life and some were even able to help their poor families they had left behind. I had a number of neighbors and relatives who had married foreigners from several different countries such as Australia, Canada, England, Germany, Belgium, and even Japan, as well as America. I had heard that many sent money back home to their families every month and I had seen boxes delivered to them full of clothing, toys, chocolates and other candies and things that made them so happy. In fact, as a little girl I had often stood out in the street and watched neighbors open boxes they had received from their foreign relative and often felt pity that my family didn't have someone who could send us boxes like that.

But the most important to me was a man with a heart who was reliable. I didn't need a man who would shower me or my family with gifts. I only wanted and hoped for a kind and gentle man who would have a heart to love me for who I am and who I could trust and count on. I would do the same for him. And I always liked the foreign-looking children. Everyone in the Philippines had black hair and dark brown eyes. I wanted a foreign child with light hair and blue eyes and I liked their light skin and thin noses. I wanted a baby who would be special in my family. This is why I had always considered marrying a foreign man. Maybe I could have a baby like so many other Filipinas who had married a foreigner and provide that child a good life with better opportunities than they would ever have in my country and maybe I could send my family a gift sometimes.

Everyone in my family accompanied me and Lonnie to the Mactan-International Airport. We arrived two hours early in order to get checked in and ready to board. In the meantime we all sat and stood around in the terminal in a little tight-net group crying and telling each other how much we would be missed. My whole family liked Lonnie already and seemed like they had a lot of respect for him. All of my family, even nephews and nieces, cried over his leaving too. My mama cried and sobbed uncontrollably the entire time.

We finally boarded a big Airbus 300 for the flight from Cebu to Manila and got buckled in. It was to be my third flight that I had ever been on. My first flight had now been over a year before when I flew to Manila with my parents for my original interview at the Embassy and then my second, of course, was with Lonnie for my second interview and medical exams. As we slowly taxied out toward our runway, I gazed out my window trying to find my family that I had left at the terminal. I thought I saw them all standing at a large plate glass window waving. I tried to hold back tears but couldn't help myself, uncertain if I would ever see them again. As the plane rumbled down the runway at full power and slowly lifted up into the sky, I attempted to hide my tears but Lonnie saw them and tried to console me. By the time we had landed in Manila, I had regained my composure—as long as I didn't think about my family—and was looking forward to my new adventure.

We had about a two hour lay-over at Manila's Aquino International Airport and my husband tried to make it interesting. We visited all of the shops in the terminal and purchased some souvenirs and then found a little café having wonderfully delicious crabmeat sandwiches. Afterwards, we boarded a monstrous Philippine Airline Boeing 747-400 for our trip to the USA. This plane was a huge double-decker with ten rows of seats across divided by two wide aisles and two large movie screens. To me, it looked more like a flying movie theater than it did an airplane—on the inside, anyway. This flight turned out to be over an eleven hour trip cruising along at about 39,000 feet.[1] We were served a very nice dinner—I chose the fish and rice and Lonnie had the chicken cacciatore—hot wash cloths to wash up prior to going to sleep, hot wash cloths to wash up upon waking up, and a great breakfast of rice, eggs, sausage, juice and coffee. Needless to say, I was greatly impressed with the meals we were getting and service we were receiving. My new American adventure was becoming quit exciting. I felt like a princess in some kind of a fairytale but I tried to control my anticipation.

My husband had once told me a story about a young teenage girl he had read about who had immigrated to America from Europe in the 1920s. Upon landing in New York City, the girl became uncontrollably hysterical upon her discovery that the city's streets weren't paved in gold as she had always heard! She had risked everything to get there. My husband did not want me to arrive in America with equal disappointment. He was always careful to teach me that America does not provide *wealth*. America provides *OPPORTUNITY*.[2]

Officially, I entered the USA on February 3, 1998. It was a very happy and exciting moment for me. For the first time in my life I had entered another country. For the first time in my life I got to see the United States of America—a place I had only known through reading, rumor, movies and TV. It was just like I was in a dream. I was also very happy and very excited about the possibility of living here but in the back of my mind I worried "what if" my husband is not what I imagined? "What if" he is not good and kind to me? I was so far from home. How could I run away and get back to my family? How could I survive and protect myself until I could find a way to return? So, as I looked around in fascination at everything so new to me, I was also praying and asking God to please watch over me and to please protect me from harm. Alternately, I was also praying to God to please make my husband as good of a person as I was led to believe that he was.

CHAPTER 10

American Arrival

According to the most recent government statistics, there are now over two-million Filipino-Americans living in the United States which is the second largest group of Asians in America, second only to the Chinese. Of that number, records compiled by the U. S. Immigration and Naturalization Service show that a total of 53,535 Filipinos immigrated to the United States during the period of the 1970s to 1980s, alone. That total ranks third among the many nations from which most U.S. immigrants have been admitted during the past two decades—preceded only by Mexico and mainland China. And where I would eventually settle with my American husband—western North Carolina—there are now more than 1,500 Filipino-American households within a fifty-mile radius.

As our plane touched down at LAX in America and we entered the terminal to stand in a long line and shuffle along to finally pass though customs, I immediately became part of those omnibus census figures.

Like so many others before me, I came to America on a hope and a prayer. I really had no idea of what to expect or what I might be heading into. I could only guess how strangely different this new land would be from the one I knew growing up and I never imagined how culturally different the two countries would be.

My husband had told me all about Los Angeles during our long flight across the ocean and I was completely convinced the city would be as warm as Manila. As we walked out of the terminal and headed for a car rental lot to get a car Lonnie had rented, we discovered LA was cold and rainy. In fact, we later learned that it was unseasonably cold in LA this particular week. Lonnie apologized for misleading me but swore Los Angeles was normally quite warm, even at night. I wasn't dressed properly for this cold so we got onto an airport shuttle bus to proceed to the car rental lot instead of walking to that location as we had intended. Loading our luggage into the car and getting in, Lonnie started the car and it surprised me. "Can you drive this?" I asked as we started to drive out of the parking space. I was somewhat worried because we had never talked about this before. I didn't know he had planned to drive a car. For some reason I just thought someone would come and get us at the airport or we would ride a cab or something like we had done all over the Philippines. "Of course," he said with a laugh. And off the lot and onto a highway we went.

It was late when we got started—about ten o'clock at night. I was getting hungry. It had been a while since our last meal on the plane and we hadn't stopped to eat in the airport. So as we drove out of the lights of LA and begin to drive into the dark across what he told me was the desert east of the city, I saw a McDonald's Restaurant. After talking about being hungry, Lonnie asked if I wanted to stop there and get something to eat. We have McDonald's in the Philippines so I recognized the restaurant very easily and thought the food would be the same but I didn't think it would be open. It was after ten but he told me this one was open 24-hours. I couldn't believe it but it was true! We went inside and there was no doubt in my mind I would order a salad. I remembered the advise of my American neighbor, Binigno Monet, and all the American magazines I had read in preparation of marrying an American, that salads were healthy for you and that is what American women concerned about their figures always ate. So, I took it all seriously and asked Lonnie to order the salad for me. When the food arrived I was shocked! I assumed I would get a salad in a little bowl but, instead, it was humongous! "This is how they watch their figures?" I thought to myself. I said nothing as I took the big bowl and we walked back to the car to continue our trip. The taste of my salad was different than I had imagined. This was a Chef Salad, with which I was unfamiliar, with eggs and meat mixed into it and a packet of some kind of salad dressing. In the Philippines our little salads are served to you already tossed, or with the dressing already mixed into it. This was an unfamiliar taste to me but I ate it anyway. I only ate one piece of the meat that I found mixed into it, however, because I discovered it was cold. In my country we don't eat cold meat. In fact, we even fry bologna, or what Americans call "lunch meat," because we think it is safer fixed that way. But I did eat the slices of eggs that were in the salad because I was familiar with them and I ate some of the vegetables, such as the cucumbers and tomatoes. I worried Lonnie would think I was wasteful but no matter how much I tried to eat, the humongous salad still looked as if I'd never touched it. I carefully and meekly told my husband I was sorry but I just couldn't finish the food. I was worried what he would say. To my surprise, he suggested I just eat what I wanted and throw the remainder away whenever we get to a place with a trash can.

Instead of being happy about his suggestion, I was mad but I remained silent. I was mad because of how easily he told me to throw it away. I thought he would volunteer to eat the rest of it like my father or brothers always did. I refused to even consider throwing this away because food in my country is hard to get. I decided I would just hold it until we got into a hotel and I would save it for later.

We proceeded on out toward my husband's Aunt and Uncle's home in Hesperia, about an hour east of L.A. We arrived late, a little after eleven, and decided to get a motel room for the night and to contact them in the morning. We got a nice room at the Red Roof Inn. Although I had spent several days in a nice luxurious hotel room at the Shangri-La Resort on Mactan Island, I was amazed at these simple, every-day motel rooms. So many people in my country would be proud to live in such a place full time. In America, even temporary accommodations were a luxury!

The following morning Lonnie called his Aunt and Uncle and we proceeded across town and met my new relatives at their house. I was scared and somewhat apprehensive but they proved to be very friendly and hospitable. Again I was amazed. They had such a nice large house for only the two of them. So much room. So much open, uncrowded space in America!

They were very kind and understanding and went out of their way to make me feel welcome. My new Aunt and Uncle—Betty and Glen—wanted to take us to a local restaurant for breakfast and Uncle Glen chose a place I had never heard of. He thought it was most appropriate, though, because it was called the *International* House of Pancakes.

After my husband's help with the menu, I ordered what I thought was a modest egg breakfast, a veggie-omelet. Uncle Glen, on the other hand, ordered what I later learned was the "full-treatment." But when my plate arrived, again I was shocked. My eyes got big and I thought, "My Lord, am I dreaming?" My omelet was huge! By my calculations my entire family could be fed breakfast from this one omelet. Again, I thought the food portions served in America was entirely too excessive but when Uncle Glen's gigantic plates of eggs, bacon, sausage, a whole stack of pancakes, several kinds of juice and a pitcher of coffee arrived at the table, I was flabbergasted! "Are these people trying to kill us," I wondered. I could not believe the amount of food brought out for one person—or that there was that much food available to begin with! Of course, Uncle Glen begin to insist I try a portion of every item he had ordered to experience the differences compared to my country. I, of course, was familiar with all of it, just not the size of the portions. The pancakes, I realized, were similar to what we call "hotcakes" in my country, which we eat as a snack instead of breakfast. I learned that in some parts of America they are also called hotcakes but in my country our hotcakes are sprinkled with powdered sugar—there is no such thing as maple syrup in the Philippines, one reason being there are no maple trees—then rolled up into a long tube-like creation with the powdered sugar on the inside, and eaten leisurely as we sit and watch TV or chat.

Since this area of California was having an unusually cold spell, after breakfast Aunt Betty, Uncle Glen and my husband all insisted we go shopping to get me a jacket, a sweater, and some additional warmer clothing such as long-sleeve blouses and some heavy slacks since I didn't have any warm clothes, and a pair of tennis or running shoes for more comfort in walking. I was wearing my only leather shoes, at the time, which were not in great condition. We went to a big K-Mart Super Store where Aunt Betty once worked and had a wonderful time walking around. Aunt Betty also insisted on buying me a plush stuffed toy and a necklace as a special gift from her and Glen.

After shopping we went back to their house and visited for a few hours. While we were there Aunt Betty offered me some chocolate candies. Chocolates are hard to get in the Philippines so, although I thought I was still possibly suffering from food intoxication from our over-whelming breakfast, I could of eaten the whole big box but I was too embarrassed so I took one or two, and then she offered me a glass of fresh milk. I begin to wonder how long I would be in America before I got too fat for my family to recognize me. I accepted the milk but I didn't like it and only had a sip or two. She might have thought I was wasteful but I wasn't used to drinking cold milk. The milk that I was used to drinking in the Philippines is served piping hot and very sweet. It's condensed milk. When I tasted the fresh cold milk I wasn't used to it and it was unsettling to my stomach.[10]

We talked and joked around until lunch time. Aunt Betty and Uncle Glen suggested we go to a Taco Bell. This was a very new experience for me, too. Lonnie ordered the food that he thought I might like because I had no idea what to get. Again, I ate a big amount of food. I ate what was ordered for me including some my husband couldn't finish because it bothered my conscience to waste any food even if it hurt my belly, because I saw in my mind's mirror the reflection of the family I had left behind who would be so very happy to have this food on their table.

Later that day, after saying goodbye, Lonnie drove down to San Diego where his brother and sister-in-law lived. They, too, proved to be very friendly and understanding but didn't seem to understand why I would marry a man Lonnie's age. My new sister-in-law, a Filipino nurse who had come to America with her parents and had lived here for years, continued to ask me many embarrassing questions, apparently in an attempt to determine if I was sincere and trustworthy.

Because the city had many shopping Malls, the next day Lonnie, again, wanted to take me shopping to build up my new American wardrobe. My new brother—and sister-in-law, Randy and Merlinda, suggested we go to a newly renovated downtown shopping center called Horton Plaza. This proved to be a very fun and entertaining experience. Horton Plaza was seven square city blocks of old historical renovated stores situated in the middle of downtown San Diego. It contained a wide variety of 140 different shops, stores, and restaurants. After hours of shopping we went to a large restaurant that I had only heard about but had never been to, Planet Hollywood. There is a Planet Hollywood in Manila, but I had never been there. Again, the portions of food were amazing as were the wide range of the offerings. I had already learned to glance around discretely whenever I was in any American restaurant to see what other people were ordering so I had some idea what to get. I had always heard it was best to look around because if a lot of others were ordering a particular item, it must be good at this establishment. Looking around, though, my heart would often ache because I would see so many people wasting so much food. I felt so guilty about all the people I had left back home who would cry for a chance to have even the scraps that remained on many of the plates as the customers got up to leave.

On the way out we decided to use the restrooms before we left. I entered the Ladies room but was immediately shocked at the extravagance. This was no ordinary CR! There were uniformed women standing all around who I later learned were "restroom attendants." After completing my duty I became frightened about what I should do or what was expected of me. I saw other women handing the attendants money for hand towels after they washed! I panicked. I had no money with me and didn't know what to do. Totally embarrassed, I rushed past them without washing and out the door. Lonnie and Randy hadn't come out of their restroom but I saw Merlinda standing in the hall. She could tell something was wrong and asked me what had happened. Reluctantly, I told her about the attendants and that I had no money. Merlinda smiled, understandably, and asked me to accompany her back to the restroom. She took my hand to comfort me and we walked back in where she tipped the lady near the sinks and we washed our hands and walked back out to the lobby, talking and laughing about the incident until our husbands came out. I just couldn't believe there were people in America who were actually paid to hand people towels in the restroom when we could just as well walk up and get our own towel. This was a strange and fascinating country I had come to.

Afterwards Randy and Merlinda took us down to the Seaport Village section of the city and we wandered along the piers and docks and shopped in the quaint little stores. I was fascinated with the beauty of the tall, cheerfully lighted down-town buildings off in the distance. I was also amazed at the rows and rows of expensive houseboats, large privately owned cabin cruisers and oceangoing speedboats docked all along the piers. Another intriguing aspect of American culture I noticed was the amount of seashells for sale in all the shops in this area. I would later notice this curious aspect in many other American tourist sites along all the beaches of this country. In the Philippines we pay little attention to the seashells and have no desire to take them home and keep them. They are all over our beaches and the shallow areas and we give them little thought. My family thought it was humorous when they saw Lonnie collect and keep a number of seashells when we were at the beach in the Philippines. On other occasions he would pay my nephews and nieces to dive down and bring him any unusual unbroken specimens from further out. I didn't realize how fascinated Americans are with seashells but, as Lonnie pointed out to me here in these shops, different varieties are offered everywhere and some command some very high prices!

The following day we went to Sea World and watched the shows. I was just as fascinated with the cleanliness of the site and the flower displays throughout the park. So much time and expense had been gone to making the whole area so attractive. I just couldn't get over it. But upon watching the seal, dolphin and killer-whale shows, I couldn't believe the amount of fish being fed to them just to perform. I noticed, too, that the fish they were using was one of my favorite and I couldn't help but think about how people I knew back home would be just as willing to do a variety of tricks for such a treat! Again, my heart felt pain and feelings of guilt crept into my mind as I watched fish being handed out to the various animals for their performance, purely for our entertainment, when I knew there were people in the Philippines who needed that food much more.

While in the park they took me to what was called Arctic Ride XD which I later learned was a *simulated* helicopter ride through the Arctic. But no one had thought to explain to me what this ride actually was or what it was about. I had been on carnival rides at various festivals in the Philippines but I had never been on a ride like this. We stood in line for a while and then entered a dimly lit room where my husband helped me buckle up a seat belt in a padded chair that I had been directed to. Then the lights went out completely and I saw on a big screen in front of us a view of the Arctic. It looked like we were walking toward a helicopter and getting into it up on the screen. Then I felt myself and my chair rise up into the air, vibrate and tilt and jerk violently back and forth and all around. I was scared and held on tight to the chair hoping I wouldn't fall or get dropped out onto the floor or maybe the high mountain that I could see in front of me and then under me. Then I felt myself go up and down and from side to side, and jerk all around as the scenery moved and swerved past me. I thought I was gonna die from a panic attack before I would be able to get out of there. Then I began to realize it was just a simulated ride sometime later. Lonnie and the others later apologized for not explaining about the ride to me before we had gotten on.

On my fourth day in America we went to the San Diego Zoo. Manila and Cebu City both have zoos but this was the biggest, most beautiful zoo I had ever attended. We saw Chinese Panda bears and Australian Kola bears and many, many other animals, all of which appeared well-fed and well cared for. In comparison to the animals I had once seen in our zoo at Cebu City, like everything else the American animals were much fatter and apparently got a lot more to eat on a daily basis than those in my country. There seemed to be much more concern for their environment here too. In America, great care and expense had been used to sanitize the animal enclosures and to make them look natural.

Our last full day in San Diego was spent shopping in the various used book stores downtown that Lonnie wanted to check out and enjoying a beautiful afternoon walking around Balboa Park and touring the Natural History Museum there. Here we saw a great display on whales from this region, rocks and minerals, and even an insect zoo.

Early the following morning Randy accompanied us to the San Diego airport where we checked in the rental car and boarded a plane for North Carolina. This was a somewhat smaller plane than we had traveled on in our flight from Manila to Los Angeles. It was about the same size plane we were on during all of our flights between Cebu and Manila.

This flight scared me. Not only was it a smaller plane but, apparently because of a severe thunderstorm, we hit turbulence over the Midwest. Lonnie held my hand and talked with me during this flight and tried to relax me and calm me down. After we landed in Greenville, South Carolina, I remained fascinated with the beauty of the airport and the surrounding countryside until we boarded an even smaller plane bound for Asheville, North Carolina, later that evening. This was what they called a "commuter" plane which only carried twenty or thirty people—more like a big taxi—and had props like an old-time airplane! This particular aircraft, barely having enough headroom for the taller people among us, provided even a scarier flight, during which it seemed to vibrate a lot and make a lot of noise as we flew along in the darkness. I was extremely happy when we finally landed in Asheville and got off that plane.

After we gathered our luggage and headed out of the terminal toward the long-term parking lot, I was struck again by the uncommonly—to me, anyway—cold weather. What few warmer clothes I had were all packed away in our luggage. Lonnie gave me his jacket to help keep me warm but it really wasn't enough. After we found his car and we got in, he handed me some kind of a little card for parking to hold onto that he had just retrieved from the console. After several attempts at turning the key in the ignition, he discovered the car wouldn't start and explained that the "battery" had apparently "died" after sitting on the parking lot in the cold winter weather for three or four weeks. Following his lead, we then got out of the car and walked back through the cold toward the terminal when he saw what he told me was an airport security officer and flagged him over. Lonnie explained to the officer what had happened and the officer told us he would meet us at the car and attempt to "jump start" it.

The car started right away and the officer refused any payment Lonnie offered for his help. I found that unusual. In my country they would expect and accept any payment for their help. Within a few minutes after starting the car and letting it warm up Lonnie asked me for the parking ticket as he started driving across the parking lot toward the exit. I told him I thought he had gotten it back earlier but he insisted he hadn't. I searched my pockets and the pockets of his jacket that I was wearing but couldn't find any ticket. Then as we neared the exit we got into our first argument. He was worried about getting out of the parking lot without the proper ticket and it upset him. I understood that, but it was the first time I had ever seen him mad and it scared me. I didn't know he was capable of being angry. He had always been so understanding and caring before.

After he had stopped at the exit toll booth and explained the loss of the ticket and then showed the airline paperwork for departure and arrival dates, Lonnie paid the parking fees and we continued on our way. As we drove some distance down the highway, however, he found the parking card in his shirt pocket. He then realized he had, indeed, originally retrieved the ticket from me shortly after having me hold onto it but due to the confusion and concern about the car not starting, he had forgotten. Lonnie was embarrassed and apologized over and over on our way to his house but it no longer mattered to me. I had already seen him mad and it frightened me.

When we arrived at his house, it was a very nice place but as he showed me around I didn't like the idea that it had a basement. I had heard stories and saw movies about basements in American homes and how people were tortured and killed in them. That scared me but I kept it to myself. I was frightened of having a house with a basement *and* I had already seen him get angry!

The next morning we awoke and I ventured out onto the deck to look around. The house was surrounded by trees! The house had a basement and was surrounded by trees! I could see a little blacktop road running past the house but I could not see any neighbors. I asked Lonnie where the neighbors were and he explained their was three other houses along the road and he pointed out their various locations through the trees where they were located. Unable to see them, I asked him when he was going to cut down all the trees. Lonnie laughed and explained that in America people paid extra for property that didn't have neighbors living close by. He told me that having privacy cost more money in America so I told him we needed to save money and have a house where I could see the neighbors.

A few days later, when I called my family, I told them all about the basement and about the trees. They, of course, began to worry too. It wouldn't be until over the next year or two that I would finally become dependent on the additional room in the basement for storage and the quiet privacy of my home's sitting that I would realize their value—once I was sure Lonnie had no deviate plans to use them against me, of course.

At first, my new home in America was much more isolated than I preferred.

I didn't have much trouble becoming accustomed to American conveniences and, in fact, Lonnie later remarked that I adapted quite quickly. Once he showed me how to use the microwave and regular ovens, the electric can opener, the dish washer, the vacuum cleaner, and all the other items, I had no trouble figuring them out for my daily use. The American TV shows that I watched or listened to as I dusted and did other chores around the house helped me to become familiar with many of the common every-day expressions, customs and slag terms in use.

One day while Lonnie was at work, out of boredom I guess, I began to snoop around in his file cabinet and found papers, pamphlets, and other information that he had been researching on the computer before going to the Philippines about the reversal of his vasectomy. That made it all come back to me and I became hurt and angry again!

But then I also found some papers, as well, which he had filled out before he had left to see me. On those papers and on a "Last Will and Testament" he gave almost all his estate to me and my family as well as to his three children. What broke my heart about this was that we were not even married yet when he had made out those papers in preparation for his long plan trip to the Philippines—which showed me that he had already placed all of his trust in me. It brought me to tears to see and read over these papers. It gave me more assurances as to what kind of a man he really was. It showed me that he really did truly love me. And because of that, I completely trusted my life to him. He didn't know that I would snoop around and find these papers in his file cabinet and had no intention of me seeing them or else the vasectomy papers would be elsewhere. After this day I knew that no amount of gossip nor any kind of rumors would ever change my mind about this man. Before this, and many times since, I have met and talked with a lot of Filipina and most of them are always suggesting that I should save some money separate from our regular bank accounts "just in case." These women give all kinds of reasons, which are very believable, of what could happen yet these people even have children together with their husbands. So, to have children together does not necessarily give you assurances at all. Many still have doubts about their husbands. For one thing, many of these women have never been listed or included on any car ownership papers, life insurance forms or home mortgage papers. I have been fortunate. Lonnie has always included me on all of those forms and, in some cases in the first few months of our marriage, insisted we include my name on all of our bank checking and savings accounts, as well as our home and car ownership papers. He even insisted that we establish additional credit in my name so that I wouldn't have problems doing so if something would ever happened to him. So, I have had my own credit cards in my own name since the first few months of my arrival in America. I have learned to trust my husband in these matters very much. Of course, I could be wrong but I have no reason to doubt his love of me.

Before I came here I thought that all the people in America were white. Many Filipinos do. They do not realize the total involvement of diversity here and that the country is made up of all the races of all the colors. When I first saw people of Mexican decent I immediately thought they were Filipinos. I have since learned we are people who probably had similar Mayon ancestry and were also ruled over by many generations from Spain. Also, as remarkable as it might sound, I had never seen a black child before coming to America! I was amazed and memorized by the first little African-American babies and children when I first saw them. I couldn't help but tell their mothers how beautiful and amazing they were as I admired and made over them in the shopping malls. The children's

Fortunately, my husband has always insisted from the very
beginning that my name be included on all of our important
papers in case anything was to ever happen to him.

parents probably thought I was crazy. There are many black-skinned people in
the Philippines, but all the ones I had seen were adults because they had come
into the larger cities, such as Cebu City, to work from nearby Negros Province.
"OH-h look Lonnie," I said upon seeing my first African-American children in
the Mall walking along with their mother, "Little Black children! Aren't they
cute," I said as I ran up and put my arm around a little boy and his sister. Lonnie
tried to quiet me down, not sure what I was going say as their mother reacted
with surprise but then smiled when she realized that I meant no harm.

Another curious aspect about where I grew up was that most Filipino people
who see a white person or Caucasian will immediately assume that the person is

an "Americano," not knowing that they might be British, German, Belgium or some other European, or perhaps Australian or from some other non-American country. We kids, and many adults, often referred to them as Joe!" or greet any Caucasians we see with "Hi Joe," as a result of believing they are Americans. The term is an old affectionate slag reference to "G.I. Joe" from WWII days that many of us grew up with or might have overheard from our parents and grandparents over the years. Although it *is* a slag term, it has never been used out of disrespect. It acknowledges the sacrifices and aid the Americans gave to our country and we use it to imply an offer of friendship or affection.

One of the first things I learned after I arrived here is that although in America there is a "freedom of religion" and a "freedom to worship," you better not talk to an American about religion or about worship. It is a subject best kept to yourself. The cruelest I was ever treated after my arrival here was when I tried to talk to my new co-workers about religion in my first American job. I don't like to dwell on this but it is important to point out, I think. I was working in a production, or assembly, line of an electronics manufacturing firm. I didn't mean anything by it and I wasn't trying to preach to them or anything. I was simply trying to create conversation and religion, to me, seemed an easy subject to talk about. Back in my country, where nearly 90% of the population is Roman Catholic and where all work and other activity stops at 3:00 p.m. to offer afternoon prayer, religion is a common, accepted, and often participated-in subject. So it just seemed natural to me to bring up the subject. Within moments, however, my co-workers not only became argumentative but in some cases angry, and one even said, "If you are so religious why did you marry an older divorced man? You'll be going to hell for that!"

I was shocked at the time and didn't understand how I had drawn so much anger from everyone over what I thought was a simple conversation about religion. I have to admit I was also deeply hurt and spent the rest of my shift with my mouth shut and tears in my eyes.

When Lonnie picked me up at work that afternoon, I was still in tears and finally broke down and sobbed as I explained to him what had happened. I didn't understand what I had done wrong and needed his help. As a result, we had a long talk that day and I learned that in America it was best not to talk about religion, abortion, or politics.

While working here I was also confronted with having to use new types of unfamiliar vending machines. I was still very naive about a lot of things in America but I didn't want people to know about it. I was still very shy at the time or had too much "hiya" to ask for help from anyone around. What I would do was quietly observe the actions of others. During my initial breaks if I wasn't sure how to use one of the snack machines I would just quietly sit at the table and keep a watch on each person as they used the vending machine until I thought I might know how. I would usually wait until no one was around to try to do it. I didn't want others watching me or perhaps make fun of me if I did it wrong or had some kind of trouble. Sometimes I had trouble and lost money or didn't get my snack and didn't know how to get my money back or where to find the return. One day I made a mistake and failed to get my snack but it just so happened that a very understanding female co-worker saw me as I started to walk away in disappointment. She asked if I needed help. I was very embarrassed but I explained my problem. She was so nice. She stood there and gave me instructions and explained to me about each machine and how to use each and what to do when each one failed or I wanted to get my money back. After her thorough instructions that day, I could always get my snacks without ever worrying about people watching me. I was so grateful for her instructions.

I was glad I had admitted my problem to her once she had asked. This was not typical Filipino behavior on my part. I guess I was becoming "Americanized"—I was succumbing to American ways. Perhaps that was good. I wasn't sure at the time but I was happy I had gotten help in this instance. Normally a Filipino, or most Asians for that matter, will refuse help when asked if they need it, usually out of pride or "hiya." The same is true with an offer of food. Their response is usually that they "have just ate" or that they "are full," even if they haven't eaten for a long time. Ask an Asian for directions, they will even smile and give you directions to someplace even when they don't really know. They are too proud or too ashamed to admit they don't know or simply don't want to hurt your feelings by not giving you some kind of directions after you went to the trouble to ask them.

I wasn't completely Americanized, however. One day at work I used the restroom and apparently I had clogged the toilet when I flushed it. I immediately ran off, out of the restroom and ignored the situation. I was too embarrassed to go tell someone so it could be fixed or cleaned up. I was afraid they would see the mess or know that I had done it so I didn't use the toilet the rest of the afternoon. Until I talked to Lonnie after I got off work, I didn't know that it was O.K. and that nobody would care that I had made a mistake.

This new life in America was going to take some getting used to.

CHAPTER 11

Typical American life of a Filipino

I stepped onto this land on February 3, 1998. When we arrived in North Carolina about a week later, it was too late for the area's annual Filipino-American (Fil-Am) Community Valentine's party. It had been scheduled a few days after my initial arrival but I was just beginning to learn all about our home, how to use all of its modern-day appliances, putting away all my stuff that I had brought with me, and I was just generally too busy getting used to my new life and all of my new surroundings so we didn't hurry around to attend.[11]

About three weeks later, Lonnie took me to my first Fil-Am Community meeting and I met many nice new Filipino friends including a number of girls and older women from my own province now living in this area. That day I met Jeanie and Genelyn who would become my best friends. They were both married to Americans and had lived in America for a year or two. They both, and a number of others in the organization, were from Cebu and we all spoke the same Visayan dialect. We spent many hours gossiping, joking around and having fun. We would spend many more hours in the following weeks and months on the telephone with each other and at other meetings. Those first few weeks, my husband also took me to a number of Carolina tourist spots, all kinds of restaurants and all the shopping malls in the vicinity. I thought I was living on the edge of paradise!

I woke up early those first mornings feeling so well, healthy and happy. It must be because I got good sleep. I begin nearly every day singing. Then I would eventually think back to the mornings in the Philippines and all the hard work we would do after we first got up. It felt so good, now, not having to do all of that. The routine I usually had in the mornings here in America was quite different. Here I would get up early and listen to the music on the radio—slow rock—as I fixed breakfast or cleaned house and then I would begin to dance for exercise as the radio stations changed their music to help make people get ready to wake up to go to work. I quickly awoke to the loud sounds of the radio and enjoyed my lively and energetic aerobic dancing. I thought all the people in America were used to it. So I sang Filipino songs in a soft voice until I became so loud and carried away that my husband would wake up and come stumbling into the room and interrupt me. It was after I had sang many songs. He told me he didn't know how I awoke so happy every morning but explained that most Americans do not do that; it can cause him a bad headache.

During that time we were still adjusting to each other. I didn't know Lonnie's normal habits well nor did he know about mine. I remember the words that many of my American co-workers used to say when we first arrived for work. "I am not a morning person," they would usually complain as they sat at the table in the break room before work, hovering over a cup of hot coffee with a terrible look on their face. I was a morning person, I guess, but by now I began to learn that Lonnie was not. On his kitchen sink was what I thought was a little toy. It was a little plastic sleepy-looking dog holding a sign "Beware of the Dog" and along the bottom of its base was the saying, "I'm not a morning person!" Now I had learned something of my husband. Perhaps the little dog was not a toy. Perhaps it was a sign for me to see. I have always continued to sing and dance in the mornings but I do it more quietly until Lonnie wakes up on his own. He often comes in to hug me in the mornings and to express his amusement of my constant cheerfulness upon waking each morning.

When I originally arrived in America at the age of 20, my English was not so good compared to Americans. Neither was my national language of Tagalog for that matter. It was true that I had been educated in English from the first grade through high school but I had seldom used it at home or in my daily life within my community. At those times we spoke our local dialect of Cebuano or Visayan. Without much need for English away from school or in some kind of professional business operation, my abilities in the language began to fade once away from school. The same was true for most of my brothers and sisters and my parents, too, of course.

My situation was not unique. Although Tagalog is the national language throughout the Philippine Islands, there are an estimated 80 different significant dialects spoken, hundreds of different local dialects and at least 32 cultural minorities throughout the country. Many of the local languages are so diverse and the communities are so isolated that a Filipino from the Visayan region of the country might not completely understand a Filipino from the Manila or the Mindanao regions. When my husband and I were in Manila, he depended on me to interpret for him when necessary. When not speaking English there, my people speak Tagalog and I understand and speak it to some extent but I am not as fluent in Tagalog as they are in Manila.

In addition to my English-language skills being out of practice, once I arrived in America I found out I had an accent that prevented many Americans from understanding what English I did use. In addition to the common inversion of our 'P' and 'F' sounds, Filipinos use vowel sounds as in the Spanish five vowel sounds without the complex and sometimes illogical phonetic variation English gives to these vowels. For instance, Americans look at me funny when I speak about the ocean beach because, to them, it sounds like I'm talking about the ocean "bitch." I speak of a sheet of paper and to them it sounds like I say "shit" of paper. There are many other words that come out differently in our pronunciation. More examples include the word "accuracy" which I and other Filipinos pronounce "ac-cure-a-cee," "calm-mit-tee," instead of "committee," "core-sage" instead of "corsage," "lay-tice" instead of "lettuce," "bird" instead of "beard," and many others. Also, a word with a double 'L' often produces a 'Y' sound in my Filipino English such as the department store Dillards which we pronounce "Dill-yards," and so on.

At the same time, although I understand English, some big complex words are confusing and some words with multiple meanings are easily misunderstand. In addition, American accents are as equally confounding to Filipinos. Most of my countrymen, including my Uncle Dictivo, maintain that Americans and Australians—and most Westerners in general—talk too rapidly through their noses while we Filipinos pronounce our English words much more succinctly through our lips.

Another observation I made immediately upon arriving in the United States was the simple fact that families in the Philippines could live off the amount of food that Americans waste and throw away. So, as my husband says, as you were growing up if your mama ever told you to clean your plate because there was a some little kid on the other side of the world who would be grateful for what you were wasting, she was telling you the truth. She was right! There were many times while growing up that I and my brothers and sisters and some of my cousins, all wished we had more to eat at any given meal. Because of that, I feel guilty about any food left on my husband's plate or my own. Therefore, nothing is ever left. I insist we either force those last couple bits down or we save the left-overs and eat them tomorrow. If at a restaurant, we bring any left-overs home to eat later. God knows, if I could send it to the Philippines, I would.

One of the most surprising aspects about our house when I first arrived was the washer and dryer. When I was a little girl growing up I truly believed that Americans were so rich they didn't have to wash their clothes. Based on all the boxes from the United States that we had seen delivered to so many Filipinos over the years, I and my cousins and all of our friends and playmates thought that people in America simply threw their clothes into a box after wearing them and, apparently, when that box was full they just shipped it all to some friend or relative in the Philippines. It wasn't until many years later, just before I got married, that I learned that this wasn't true. I still wasn't convinced that washing our clothes in a machine in our house or not hanging them out to dry in the sun was sanitary. It took my husband weeks to convince me this was OK. Once I realized the clothes were "comparably" clean and sanitary doing them this way and the fact it was much easier than the way it had to be done in the Philippines, I became quite used to it and preferred it. Still, it was somewhat disappointing to lean we couldn't just throw our dirty clothes in a box, buy new ones, and ship all of our old ones to my family. They would love them.

Clothes that bore tags of an American manufacturer were highly sought in my country and were the most prestigious clothing items one could have—whether used or not. Once I got to America, I was shocked to find so much clothing sold in the malls that bore a "Made in the Philippines" tag. I just couldn't get over the fact for a long time that I had traveled 7,000 miles to buy new clothing that I could of purchased in my own country—and purchased it there a lot cheaper!

Another surprising aspect I learned about the American culture is that it is such a litiginous society. In the Philippines we settle our disputes among ourselves. Normally, the other person is willing to work things out—even if reluctantly—and it is not until they stop or refuse to cooperate that we find it necessary to contact an attorney. Nor do we expect anything more than we need to take care of the problem. In the Philippines the people do not seek or expect compensation for "punishment" or for "pain and suffering." I remember one time my little brother Richein bit down on a sewing needle that had apparently fallen into the bread dough of our neighborhood bakery. He was probably four or five years old at the time. One morning while we were all eating fresh rolls at breakfast, Richein started screaming and crying and Mama found a little needle stuck in the roof of his mouth. Mama and Papa rushed him to the doctor to get him treated and taken care of and then proceeded directly over to the little bakery shop and confronted the owner. There was no suing or threats of suing. When confronted, the family that owned and operated the bakery apologized repeatedly and agreed to pay all of the doctor's bills. Another time, when Richein was even younger, he was following me down the street one evening and apparently walked out in front of a motor-trike after I had crossed the road. He got run over and laid in the street screaming and yelling as everyone gathered around helping him. Mama and Papa were notified and came running down the street too. After a cursory examination Papa found no serious injuries—only a few minor cuts, scratches and bruises. The motorcycle driver and his passengers told Mama and Papa what had happened and continued on their way. There was no suing or threats of suing. In fact, as my parents led us away toward our house to attend to Richein's wounds, they told me it was all my fault for not watching out for my poor little brother.

Us kids were always getting hurt out playing. The Philippines is formed mostly of coral and volcanic rock. Every time we ran and fell down it was like falling on a patch of porous cinders. As a result, few of us grew up without scars. Our parents used herbs and leaves to relieve pain and prevent infection as did all the parents in our neighborhood. We weren't taken to the doctor or hospital for every injury nor did we blame our neighbors for accidents on their property. We played throughout the neighborhood and sometimes one kid was responsible for someone falling down and getting injured but we just took it in stride. One kid might get mad at another about it but the parents didn't get involved or threaten with lawsuits. It was just part of life. Things just happen and we all realized that.[12]

One of the most surprising or scary aspects I learned about America was about its cars. In my county public transportation was so easy and convenient. A motor-trike from my Gun-ob neighborhood to Lapu-Lapu City, where we could go to a variety of stores, city hall, the post office, or a taxi-terminal, cost us about P2. A taxi-cab from Lapu-Lapu City to Cebu City was about P20 to P25 and the same amount to return. There are also a wide array of jeepneys, vans and buses always available throughout the towns and the cities costing only a few centavos to ride.[13] An over-whelming number of these vehicles are available everywhere and at all hours of the day or night. In addition, neighborhood stores having most necessities are available all around us within walking distance. We Filipinos can go our whole lives without ever having to learn to drive.

But I soon learned that in the USA a car is a necessity. One has to learn to drive to get around because *nothing* is within walking distance. One morning my husband decided to teach me how to drive. While the car was parked in our driveway he went to the left door and opened it. He instructed me to get in and do things like get situated in the driver's seat, start the car, turn the headlights on, use the turn signals and beep the horn. Then he instructed me on how to use the accelerator and shift the gear lever into the reverse position. He then told me to gently step on the gas pedal and back the car slowly down the driveway. The next thing I know, the car went BAM, KAPOW, and Lonnie fell to the ground. I had knocked him down as I backed up quickly and caught him before he could get out of the way of the open car door. I became a nervous wreck and started to cry. I was too shook up to do anything. As he slowly climbed back to his feet, using the hood and left fender of the car for support, he told me to move the transmission lever back into the "Park" position and to turn it off. I did as he instructed and got out of the car, standing next to it and continued to cry. I didn't know what to do. I didn't want to drive any more. Surprisingly, Lonnie wasn't mad. He kept telling me it was alright and not to worry about it. He told me it was his fault for not paying more attention to what he was directing me to do or for not realizing what would happen. He wasn't mad. I guess he was just happy to be alive and unhurt. During another driving lesson a few days later, I backed and turned too sharply out of our driveway and we ended up in a ditch at the bottom of a short embankment. Luckily neither of us were hurt and there was no damage to the car but it was wedged into the ditch and had to be lifted back onto the road by a tow truck. Lucky, too, Lonnie had AAA coverage so even the tow truck coming out to our house didn't cost us anything.[14]

I wanted him to just buy me a bike or a moped for my transportation but he told me the traffic moves much too fast in America to be driving such vehicles along the roads. He explained that they are quite appropriate in Philippine traffic but in this country cars are speeding past you at 55 or 60 miles an hour and it is too dangerous for people on bikes or mopeds. He was right. Several months after my request, a teenager in our community was hit by a car while driving a moped and lost both of his legs. Some months later I heard on the TV news of a traffic accident and death involving a bicyclist.

Lonnie insisted that I would have to learn to drive a car. After several weeks of him giving me driving lessons the best he could, he admitted his nerves were "shot" and he found it too frustrating. He arranged for lessons through a commercial instructor listed in the phone book.

This man—the instructor—proved to be totally unreliable. After several weeks of driving lessons, he began giving me a kiss on the check and praising my driving at the end of each lesson as he dropped me off at my house. I wasn't sure about American ways but I didn't like this. It made me extremely nervous and it didn't seem right. I asked Lonnie about it and he agreed. After we talked about how wrong this was, Lonnie called him and told him that I wanted to stop the lessons and to simply mail my paper work to us. When the guy insisted on being told why I wanted to quit, Lonnie told him it was because of his insistence of kissing me at the end of each lesson. He admitted he had but insisted he meant nothing by it and I had no reason to be upset to which Lonnie remarked "I'll bet you don't kiss your male students at the end of each lesson." The guy was mumbling as Lonnie hung up. Within days my paperwork arrived showing that I had passed my Driver's Training and passed all exams.[4]

After several more weeks of driving practice with Lonnie, I went for my driving exam. I passed the written test with no problem but when I went out on the actual driving test with the examiner, I "rolled" through every stop sign I came up to. The examiner said nothing until the end when he told me that I had flunked because I had never actually stopped at any of the stop signs. I was embarrassed but Lonnie told me on the way home that it was actually his fault because that is how he drives and he never thought to tell me any different during our practice. A month more of driving practice and learning to bring the car to a complete halt at all the stop signs and I went for another exam. This second time I passed and was proud to receive my new driver's license. Later that evening I called my family in the Philippines and told them all about the tests and how I was now able to drive. I worried my Mama and Papa when I insisted that I would rent a car and take them for a ride on my next visit to the Philippines. Mama "thought" it would be OK but Papa kept telling me it wouldn't be necessary.

Happy to have my driver's license, this is the
photo of me in my new car that I sent to my family.

When I was growing up in my country I thought I had a very difficult, very hard life. Our daily chores were all accomplished by arduous manual labor. Even just to have water we had to work hard by pumping it from a well and carrying it to the house in a heavy bucket. Papa or one of my older brothers usually took care of this but there were times I had to do it myself. By the age of six I was expected to start helping my mom and dad. My chores at that time were to watch my little baby brother while mom washed our clothes and to watch him while she cooked our meals and cleaned our house. Some mornings I was assigned the additional duties of sweeping the ground where the leaves had fallen or to pick up all the trash or plastic wrap that people had thrown down as they had passed by on the street or the wind had blown into our yard. Some mornings I was also assigned to water the plants but usually my two older brothers were assigned to this detail. Most of the other time throughout the day I was assigned to act as a handyman for my mother by going off to get things for her like to run off to the one of my aunt's houses to borrow something or to run down to a nearby convenience store to get 1-peso-worth of oil or to get one or two eggs. We would do these kind of chores and errands every day—if not in the morning, then maybe around noon or perhaps at night. Our chores grew as we all got older. In my kid or adolescence period, those were my chores. As I got older, perhaps between ten and twelve, I learned to cook the rice and I was expected to have a pot of it ready by the time the rest of the family had finished their chores and had sat down for breakfast, lunch or dinner. Unfortunately, I usually got complaints from some member of the family and sometimes from all the members. It seems the rice I fixed was always either in need of more water according to some of my family members—too hard or not moist enough, according to others—or it had too much water according to still others. And a few times *everyone* in the family complained because I had burned it.

At an older age I was expected to help stock some water in the big barrel outside the house for mom to wash our clothes, help her hang the clothes on the clothes line and then help her gather the clothes after they had dried. During all of these chores we talked of various things together as we worked and gossiped and joked and as we folded the clothes the way Mama liked. My sisters were often assigned to help too. There were so many clothes to wash every day that there was always plenty for all of us to do. My sisters and I were also alternately assigned to help Mama wash dishes after every meal and as we got older Mama stopped and we girls were assigned individually to that chore. Other sideline chores of mine in my early years involved helping my grandfather. My poor Lolo had been blind my entire life so it was never new to me. I helped him walk to the CR every morning. He would use me as his cane by holding onto my shoulder as he walked along. I would also pump a bucket-full—probably two or three gallons—of water at the well for him to use and carry it over to the CR. This was for him to wash up with and to flush his toilet. In the early days before my Papa took over, I would also help Lolo go to his work at the fishpond whenever Mama told me to. This was about a five mile walk from our house. I would also accompany him to his army veteran meetings in Lapu-Lapu City every month. Because of my husband's interest in history, he has often asked me what they had talked about at those meetings but I truly do not remember because my only interest was in eating the free snacks that was offered there. They would often have such things as a little slice of white bread containing a sandwich spread, wrapped in tissue paper, and a coca-cola. I was thrilled. That is the part of it that I remember! I looked forward to attending those Veterans' meetings. We also often went to Mandaue City to see his political friends. Basically, I guess, I was his first choice of a companion and helper if grandmother or his youngest son was not available.

So now I have the experience of living in two different worlds or cultures. Yes, the Philippines has a lack of many conveniences and a lot of hard labor jobs in many instances, including even in housework, compared to America but many Filipinos have it easier—in my opinion—if they have foreign relatives because of the bayanihan and the thousands of dollars sent to them or the help often provided whenever they have a problem.[5] In America we have to take out a loan, file an insurance claim, or in some way rely solely on ourselves and our finances whenever unexpected problems come up. To be sure, Filipinos are very appreciative and very happy when they are helped or receive money from their relatives living in America or when you can provide them with enjoyable simple luxuries such as Tanduay rum, mongo beans and pansit and special snacks like biko and rice cakes but America is very difficult to live in. There is nobody to do errands for you or to make you happy with free things or special needs like in the Philippines nor is there anyone you can give orders to for help without payment. You have to know a lot of things, to rely upon yourself, it seems to me, in order to survive in America. Like when something goes wrong with your car, your house, your health, or whatever, because every move you make—every problem that comes up—costs a fortune to repair or make right in America! Yes it's nice to have a car but the cars are very expensive to buy, it is absolutely mandatory to have your car and your driving covered by adequate insurance—which is also costly each month—and the gasoline and monthly maintenance costs are also expensive. The same is true of having a house. Initial cost, monthly mortgage payments, insurance payments, upkeep and maintenance costs are not realized, thought about or understood by the average Filipino. Most people in my country do not understand this or realize how expensive it is. Many Filipinos think that if you own a house and a car, you must be rich. They simply do not realize the monthly expenses of up-keep, loan payments, insurance costs, and all the other expenses that are involved with such ownership. I didn't realize it myself until I moved to America and took on the responsibilities of such things. I was lucky my husband knew a few things about buying and owning homes, owning cars, and the need for me to establish credit in my own name. We are not rich but we are doing OK. Then again, compared to a third-world country like I came from, I guess we are rich. But it just seems it is all relative. The more you have, the more you have to spend. No matter where you live, you still have worries about bills, credit and money. It just varies to what degree you owe your creditors. In America we have the opportunity to obtain a lot more but we have a lot more credit—a home mortgage and financed cars—debts uncomprehensible to the average Filipino. In the Philippines we often owed for our daily necessities such as for the vegetables we got from our neighborhood vendor or for our monthly electric bill or our weekly propane tank needs for cooking. By American standards what we owed or needed each month to pay our bills wasn't much, but by Philippine standards, it sometimes caused us a terrible worry. It's all relative!

But as I came to America, I apparently carried all kinds of guilt with me. Every time we went to a fancy restaurant I always saw my life back home—as if there was a magic mirror that made me look back at myself, my life growing up, and my family's situation. I know my husband probably got tired of hearing it all the time but so many times as we ate I always had a flashback and started telling him that the food we were just served was so much that we could feed from three to five people with it in my family. I felt guilty. I had so much food and my brothers and sisters, and my parents, probably had very little that day. I couldn't get through a meal without such thoughts and I couldn't bear leaving any leftover food on the table. I would take it home and put it in our refrigerator and I would always eat it the following day.

At the same time, I was very conservative in fixing meals at home to make sure I didn't waste any of our food or make too much for the two of us. Lonnie often teased me about the sandwiches I would fix for him to take to work. He would open the sandwich and find I had placed one ultra-thin slice of Buddig meat—wafer-thin—between two slices of bread with mayonnaise sparingly spread on one side. After a couple of these he insisted I make the sandwiches thicker and with more mayonnaise. For several days I increased the meat by perhaps two or three slices and he finally had to show me how he used a half-package of meat for each sandwich. It took me a long time to be able to make his sandwiches like that. I had to work my way up to it by adding a slice or two each time. He was very patient and sort of got a kick out of it, I guess.

But in other ways I was not as conservative as I should have been. Filipinos are very brand-name and country conscious. Even the poorest of us prefer a brand-name product over a cheaper off-brand and if we can't afford the famous brand or an item "Made in America," then we prefer just to do without. This, too, is a matter of pride I guess. Even in the restaurants I often chose what looked the best or what I wanted the most with complete disregard of the price. The same held true with clothes. I kept reflecting back on my life and how it was for me in the Philippines and telling myself to get over my ego. "Someone who couldn't afford things in the past," I kept telling myself, "should not desire the best of everything now. I should be happy with anything luck has provided." I knew I was getting carried away because I was always feeling guilty afterward for ordering the expensive food, buying the expensive clothes and looking at the brand name without ever first looking at the price. I went through a spell where I would talk my husband into buying a particular dress, blouse, or shoes and then, without him ever saying a word, feel guilty about it for days until I talked him into taking me back to the store to return the item. It was like an uncontrollable obsession. "Perhaps I am getting like Imelda Marcos," I sometimes thought. "Perhaps that is what caused her obsession with clothing and shoes that Americans find so humorous. She obsessed for, as an adult, what she had grown up without!"

I honestly knew I was becoming a brat, a phony or some kind of a braggart during my first few months in the U.S.A. There were times I thought about it and was ashamed. My husband spoiled me those first few months. He would let me do whatever I wanted or buy nearly everything I desired just to make me happy.

He showed me nice things and nice places as much as he could and he gave me a good quality time Then the day finally came when he sat me down and talked to me about choosing whether I wanted to keep buying so much clothing and nice things for myself or if I wanted to help support my family. I dearly loved all the nice clothing and I really liked spending money on myself but I also worried about my family and felt guilty about their needs. He told me we could continue in our lives doing one or the other but we could not afford to do both.

I understood and after that day I began to change my attitude. Perhaps I simply just grew up and matured.

Another problem I had back then was "Chocolate!" Oh my gosh! I don't know how I could eat so much candy without gaining hundreds of pounds and getting fat. It seems a problem to me now and I dance and exercise to keep fit and eat it in moderation but for the first few months after my arrival in America I ate plenty of it. Back home candy was very hard to get. My parents often had to choose between candy for their children or being able to afford a "partner" for the rice. They seldom got us candy except during special occasions or for holiday celebrations. Even in those times we only got a few pieces each. Four little pieces of candy cost one peso but it could often leave an empty place in our stomach when that one peso was enough to provide a rice partner of approximately three tablespoons of salted shrimp paste, a small anchovy-size salted fish, a salted mussel or two pieces of dried fish. A family of eight can eat a peso's worth of those choices and have a happy stomach.

Sometimes we kids would buy a little bit of candy on our way to school instead of using it to purchase a school supply that was needed or to buy a good nutritious snack during our first break. I can remember occasionally finding a little wrapped piece of hard candy as I was walking along the street and be so happy and excited that I would pick it up, brush it off, unwrap and eat it and feel so lucky.

At the same time, chocolate was difficult to get in the Philippines when I was growing up. It was expensive when it was obtained. So when I arrived in the U.S.A. and chocolate was so inexpensive and everywhere, I went through a spell where I wanted as much of it as I could get as often as I could get it. Again, probably as a result of doing without and obsessing for it as I was growing up.

I was equally amazed at the cakes in America, chocolate or otherwise. They were all so-o-o-o moist and easy and convenient to get here. In America you can buy a cake anytime. You can eat it as a dessert during your lunch, after your supper, or just as a snack. In America cakes are as easy to get as candy and you don't have to wait until your birthday. In my country cakes and candy were both difficult to get, even a little piece, because they were both rare and expensive. Cakes, however, were even more rare and expensive because of the necessity of requiring milk, flour, sugar, and a stove to prepare it. You just can't prepare a cake over an open fire or on a hot plate like most of the Filipinos are limited to.

One aspect of America that I didn't appreciate was the availability of medicine here. When I first arrived in America I was appalled at the amount of advertizing on the T.V. and in magazines, billboards, and everywhere else enticing us all to take pills—for headaches, for stomach aches, for menstruation pain, to go to sleep, to stay awake, to calm down, to pep up, for anything and everything. I was convinced this was wrong and didn't trust any of the claims or see why it was necessary to use to begin with. I trusted the natural medications my parents had provided me as I was growing up and had learned from my parents that the basis for most modern-day medications were the herbs, leaves and bark we had always used to begin with.

From the beginning my husband used care and understanding but tried desperately to steer me away from herbal medicine, claiming modern American medicines were more advanced and quicker acting. He maintained they were improvements of their basic herbal ingredients. Still, I clung to my original beliefs because I was more comfortable with what I had grown up with and had become accustomed to since my childhood. I was also more comfortable with not taking pills for every ailment like so many Americans seem to depend upon. For instance, I still prefer Efficascent Oil to be rubbed on my abdomen instead of Pepto-Bismol taken internally for gas or for a stomach ache. It seems more reasonable to me. Likewise, asuti leaves instead of Midol for menstral cramps seemed to have worked much better in the past. I do take aspirin when absolutely necessary and have since gradually resorted to using cold tablets, Thera-Flu, Alka-Seltzer or Ny-Quil on occasion as a last resort.

Probably the most valuable lesson or observation I have made about this country, however, is that America truly is a land of opportunity. It is a place to find your self-esteem. It is a place to dream. It is a place to create your future. In my country ordinary people are not allowed to excel. There, you are expected to remain whoever or whatever you were—whatever your position was—when you were born. They will always insist that you are too short, too fat, too ugly, too old or have no brain—perhaps like my teachers or my parents often told me: that I had a brain like an anchovy—very small. If your family is not wealthy, you are constantly reminded by others that you can not do certain things and that you are better off not to try. So you spend nearly all of your time taking care of your family, looking for rice, looking for ways to afford rice, looking for twigs and leaves as fuel to cook the rice and looking for food-partners to go with your rice. And that becomes your entire life. In my country—in many third-world countries—for many of us, that is what we have to look forward to in our future.

CHAPTER 12

Holiday Differences and how they are observed

After about five or six months in America, those feelings of home-sickness that I had been repressing since I first arrived here slowly began to make an appearance. I finally realized how much I missed my parents, my brothers and sisters, all of my aunts and uncles, all my little nephews and nieces, my neighbors and my neighborhood, my small town, my former friends, my former co-workers, my entire country and my former life. Each night more memories and sadness hit me. I cried myself to sleep for several nights. Lonnie felt helpless trying to comfort me. Nothing could stop the flow of tears. At church one Sunday morning, an older Filipino women who attended there all of a sudden reminded me of my mother and I began to sob uncontrollably. She and others tried to console and comfort me—and that was during the regular church services. Guessing by the looks we got from some of the people around us, there were probably those in church who thought my tears and uncontrollable crying was really a result of my "older" husband having somehow abused me or that he had been preventing me from contacting my family. But nothing could be farther from the truth. I had called and talked with my Filipino family, at Lonnie's encouragement, nearly every other week during that time. Those first few birthdays of all of my family members that I had missed and the approaching holidays were probably what stirred up my original feelings of homesickness. In the Philippines there is much more emphasis—much more importance—placed on celebrating one's birthday. The whole family participates in one another's birthday. We don't just go out as a couple for a nice romantic dinner. In the Philippines it is a big deal! We are celebrating our "Natal Day," the day that God first gave us life in this world! It is a day to celebrate, commemorate, and observe. My family could never afford to give a big gift or some fancy birthday cake to any of us kids but I don't ever remember a time when we didn't have the big birthday-food celebration—the pansit and the biko. Mom sometimes would tell me she "just couldn't prepare the food for my birthday" or she would say I didn't deserve to have a big birthday dinner because I did not meet a lot of her expectations during that particular year but she often did that as a joke. Or some of my brothers or sisters would come and tell me they had overheard Mama and Papa saying "we had no food for Melba's birthday" but I would find out that was a joke too.

At each of our birthdays, Mama and Papa would be up early to prepare the feast. By dawn Mama would just be coming home from the market with the fresh vegetables, seafood and spices. Papa would already be cooking up a big kettle of biko over an open fire in the yard just outside our house. Every one of our birthday celebrations had to have an unlimited supply of biko—a sweet mixture of glutenous rice or millet, brown sugar and coconut milk, all cooked together and when served having a texture similar to the American treat of chocolate brownies but the appearance of rice crispies. We also always had plenty of *tikoy*, sweet rice cakes. Both, being sweet and sticky, was to symbolize the closeness of the family. The pansit—a combination of cooked shredded lettuce and other vegetables, shredded chicken and rice noodles—was to symbolize a long life as evidenced by the long noodles. By mid morning all of our Aunts, Uncles, cousins and many neighbors and other acquaintances arrived to take part in the celebration and feast. At our birthday parties no one brings gifts—nor are they expected to. They simply bring their appetite and best wishes for you. Sometimes someone might bring a simple gift. If they do, in my country, we do not open any gifts until after everyone leaves. It is our custom to only open gifts alone to prevent embarrassing those who couldn't bring gifts or to prevent anyone from comparing who brought what or whose gift was more expensive or less expensive. That is our way. Again, it involves *hiya* and the preservation of pride.

My first fancy birthday cake, a sheet cake made at one of our local bakeries in Lapu-Lapu City, was purchased by Lonnie and we have since provided a cake for each of my brothers and sisters on their birthday just so they could have the experience. Proudly, ever since then, my parents have been able to provide a fancy birthday cake for many of my nephews and nieces—their grandchildren—on their birthdays as well as the normal birthday fare of pancit and biko.

Christmas in the Philippines is different too. Back in my country we put up our Christmas trees and decorations as early as November 2—the day following All Saints Day—and leave them up to as late as mid-January. Radio and TV stations begin playing Christmas tunes as early as that date, too, while the various personalities begin counting off the days until the holiday as they open their show or sign on each morning. By the first week of November most people have put up their Magay tree—a tree that grows abundantly in swampy areas and normally has many small branches. Some Filipinos use the Bakhaw—a type of small mangrove tree—instead. Either of these trees are usually obtained as early as September in anticipation of the holiday and given time to dry out.

Then around November 2 or 3 we put our tree in a big container, such as a Nido milk powder can or something similar, fill it with small stones to keep the tree upright, and place it all in a corner of our front room. We then wrap each little branch with green, white or red crinkled tissue paper—which we call Japanese paper but what Americans call crepe paper—and decorate it in more detail with handmade ornaments made of paper or foil, candies and lollipops. We also sometimes whipped up soap detergent into a white foam and spread that on our little tree. Once the foam dried, it looked like snow on our tree—snow on a Christmas tree in the Philippines!

Afterwards, the various candies hanging from the branches were often replaced with small stones or large seeds during the night. As each day passed, the tree was decorated by less candy and more stones, which often angered Mama. It seemed she would always blame me or accuse me of replacing the candy with the stones while everyone slept. It never mattered how much I denied any involvement, but Papa and my brothers and sisters always remained quiet and let me take all the blame!

Nine days of Catholic masses, held at 4-a.m. each morning, begin on December 16 through December 24. Christmas lights and star-shaped lanterns, called *parols*, are often arranged in all the windows of homes and stores and, under Philippine law, every working person is supposed to have ample financial resources during the Christmas season. As a result, by the 20th of December at the latest, a bonus equivalent to one month's salary is added to every employee's pay and the shopping centers begin holding all-night Christmas sales soon afterwards that continue through December 24. Nearly all other big businesses and manufacturing plants close from December 20th to the end of the year and all mail delivery stops from December 15 to January 2 in observance of the holiday. Many working people have this time as their only vacation opportunity and pack up to go to other areas to visit friends or relatives for the holidays. Relatives from the mountain barrios often come down to visit and stay with relatives in the bigger towns and cities and it is not unusual to be visited by relatives and cousins we haven't seen in years. The country and nearly all major commerce comes to a complete standstill during much of this period. Sending out Christmas cards is not a common observance in the Philippines anyway. We do sometimes give out an occasional Christmas card to our friends at school, a neighbor, or to someone special in our lives but the sending out of cards is not a widely practiced affair as it is in America. On the other hand, Christmas caroling is very common in the Philippines and is eagerly participated in—again beginning as early as November. Groups of children and teens go around the neighborhoods caroling from door to door for small amounts of money handed out. At the end of the evening the children divide any money that they have collected and use it to buy candy for themselves and their family to help celebrate the holidays. Because of a lack of money for many in our neighborhood a few people would, instead of money, hand out homemade deserts such as sweet rice or coconut cookies while others, like my family sometimes, would reluctantly have to turn out their lights and pretend to be asleep when they heard carolers coming down the street because they didn't have any money to give. Not unlike any other country, there is also a Christmas "scrooge" or two in nearly any neighborhood who will give us what we called "a pee shower"—throwing the contents of their chamber pot out the window at us or sometimes just a bucket of water to make us think it was pee—because they didn't want to be bothered by our singing and merriment or perhaps because they'd had an unusually sad life. Others might even treat us like a dog if they didn't like our singing. They would "shoo" us away saying, "Your voice sounds like a barking dog, go away!"

But, of course, for the most part we all enjoyed caroling throughout the neighborhoods and even laughed or teased each other about the times we were chased or driven away from some homes.

When I first came to America I was amazed at the out-and-out commercialism of Christmas. In the Philippines it is a very religious holiday. In fairness though, Filipinos do sometimes exhibit a similar *pasaway* or shallowness—like during the baptisms of their children they will often choose or name a lot of "sponsors" and godparents who are wealthy, or well-off, for their child in the hope that the sponsor or godparent will be generous as the years pass. This is most evident on birthdays and holidays. In fact, Filipino children depend more on gifts from their godparents than they do on their own parents. During Christmas the children will often receive all kinds of gifts from their godparents. In my family, all of my brothers and sisters had several sponsors and godparents except for me. I only had one sponsor at my baptism but she was supposedly a very wealthy lady. For some reason, however, she later ran off never to be seen again.

Just my luck as a child, I guess. I was the only one in my family not to have a godparent to visit during Christmas while each of my brothers and sisters had anywhere from five to ten. So every Christmas I felt a little sadness and experienced a little envy toward my brothers and sisters. They received all kinds of gifts, from money to clothing, while I was left hoping Mama could afford to have something for me, either a tee-shirt with printed advertisement from a store supplier she had patronized or something special she had received from a supplier. I often accompanied my brothers and sisters as they visited their godparents and watched them collect their gifts. I was always envious of Rechien who had several very generous godparents. Sometimes they would pity me and hand me a few pesos or a little gift when I went with him. So would some of the others when I went with one of my other brothers or sisters. If our family was fortunate during the year and mom had a little money to spare—and if she had liked what I had accomplished—she would buy some clothing material and let me decide what style of dress I wanted her to make for me or sometimes she would just surprise me with a ready-made dress. Unlike America, children in the Philippines have always *loved* to get clothing for Christmas presents. Those were my favorite Christmases. And I always looked forward to my father's gift from his boss when he was working the fishpond because his boss always provided for our whole family at Christmas. He would give us anywhere from three to five large packages of hard candy and a tin full of cookies. Often this was a large can of shortbread or sugar cookies with various kinds of sprinkle toppings. I loved those and they would be divided up and distributed among us children and the close relatives by Mama on Christmas morning. My father also often received some hand-me-down clothing from his boss' son at Christmas which usually included some jeans, a good shirt or two, a pair of shoes and four brand new tee-shirts. The latter went to Dad, Mom, Carlito and Ferdinand. The rest of us would get the candy and cookies and then Dad would go out and get some fresh fruits for us as additional gifts. Of course, we would all look forward to a big meal that he and Mama would fix for our whole family and any other of our relatives who visited us on Christmas day.

In the Philippines, the Christmas-day meal is the main event—the major gift—that the parents provide their children. By afternoon, additional relatives and neighbors often come together to eat and exchange gifts of candy. Much like what Americans call a pot-luck dinner, these families bring different dishes so that we get to experience the "specialities" of others. The gifts exchanged are quite often homemade gifts and the children then all gather outside under a tree to try and break a *palayok*, or what Americans know as a pinata, that is full of candy and coin-money.

Another common Philippine custom during the Christmas season is for the girls and women to wear a polka-dot dress at New Years. A polka-dot dress is for good luck and prosperity in the New Year. The numerous "dots" are suppose to symbolize coin-money.

New Years eve in the Philippines is sometimes very dangerous. Many Filipinos celebrate by shooting off fireworks and guns into the air. Unlike America, there is no limit to the size or power of the fireworks and every year thousands are killed and maimed by the celebrating explosions and the falling spent bullets, not to mention the sometimes terrific fires that result. Such coverage dominates our T.V. news from several days before New Years to several days after. At midnight, members of the family gather to ring in the New Year with good-luck customs and the traditional *media noche*, or midnight meal. At the stroke of 12:00 every one in the family cheer and hug one another and march around the house, entering every room downstairs and upstairs, banging pots and pans and shaking tin-cans full of coins making a loud racket to frighten away any evil spirits or bad luck in the house. Meanwhile, many of our neighbors run their motorcycle up and down the street with a lot of cans dragging behind to make a lot of loud noise out in the streets. Once we have made several laps through our house making the noise, the family sits down to a fine meal consisting of pansit—or spaghetti, if *that* can be afforded—to promote a long life, plenty of rice, to insure that the family will not go hungry and will have plenty throughout the year, any kind of beef dish, to insure that everyone in the family will be hard-working throughout the year like the carabao—absolutely no chicken dishes so the family will not be "scratching" out a living and no pork dishes to insure that no one in the family will be lazy or lay around like a pig—any kind of shrimp dish and plenty of fish, to insure an "active," prosperous year, a wide selection of fruit, which is a symbol of good health and wealth in the New Year, and a big dish of *biko*, the sweet brown-sugar rice-cake desert, to promote closeness—or stickiness—and sweetness among the family members throughout the year.

In the area of the Philippines where I was born and raised, three weeks after our New Year celebration, the great *Sinulog* festival takes place. This is an annual event that takes place on the Third Sunday of January. It is the holiday climax of the week-long observance of *Pasundayag sa Sinulog*. At noon, a great and nearly hour-long parade begins as gaily decorated floats covered in flowers and orchids and throngs of costumed people, marching, dancing and singing, make their way through the streets of Cebu City. The participants all dance down the streets using a unique Sinulog step, singing and accompanied by a shrill, rhythmic whistle blast accompaniment and shouting "Pit Senyor," meaning "*viva el Senor*," or "long live Santo Nino"—the child Jesus. According to my husband, this great Filipino celebration event would be similar to the Mardi Gras parade held in the American city of New Orleans each year—but without the sexual overtones.

We celebrate St. Valentine's Day much as it is done in America. Every girl or boy gives a card to everyone who is special to them. We buy cards in the store or we make them at home to give out to those who are special in our lives. Flowers are often given too but there is not as much emphasis on giving candy or chocolate as there is in America. Still, small gifts and cards are personally delivered or sent and many couples dress up to go to nice restaurants, dance in the discos or go to the movies. You can easily identify the men or women who have no sweetheart that day because they will wear something prominent in the color red which signifies they are available or need a partner. Like in the West, however, many Filipino weddings are also scheduled on this day.

Easter is an intensely religious period of observance in the Philippines. Maundy Thursday, Good Friday and Easter Sunday are all official holidays. It is sadly observed as "the day God died" and on Maundy Thursday all the shops close, nearly all the traffic stops, and silence reigns throughout the country as people somberly attend church. Even Philippine Airlines' flights stop and do not resume until Saturday in observance of the period. Beginning that Thursday night, and every evening afterwards, processions of people, many carrying floats containing statutes of "Mama" Mary, Joseph, Jesus, and various Saints, walk through the neighborhoods gathering additional followers as they go and reciting the Stations of the Cross and the Rosary. On Easter morning, before dawn, every neighborhood church presents a widely attended Passion Play at the end of the procession and then at dawn everyone attends Mass.

The day of June 12 is observed as our Philippine Independence Day from Spain and is a National Holiday marked by military parades and family activities or simply as a day of rest and relaxation. No fireworks are used to mark our Independence Day, as is done in America. In the Philippines, fireworks are used only in the observance of New Years Day and, to a lessor extent, to celebrate the birth of Christ on Christmas. For a number of years our Independence Day was held on July 4 in the Philippines because that is when the country was granted independence by the United States in 1946, however, that date is now simply referred to as Philippine-American Friendship Day and is barely noted by anyone now except in the schools, in the business world, and by the many Philippine-American pen-pals. In fact, several times over recent years, postage stamps have been issued in the observance of the day for use in the mails.

In my area of the country June 29 is observed as the Feast of the Two Saints, St. Pablo and St. Juan,[1] and is marked by early worship at the church and family gatherings. In addition, the month of June is officially the month for families to gather at the beach for swimming and picnicking. For me, this was a family tradition. We would always go to the beach after church that day and have what Americans would refer to as a picnic, But the date of June 29 is also the day great crowds of people show up at the beaches, especially the sick and infirm, because it is a day widely believed to be when the water is miraculous and will help the ill and the crippled. The people will do all kinds of tricks just to get you wet that day and you have no choice but to get drenched. Especially if a person appears as though they have not had a bath in a long time. People will grab them off the street and they are likely candidates of getting dunked in water. I have no idea how or who started this tradition in the Philippines but my sister Helen has since told me that maybe it is from the Bible and the mention of Saint John's baptism of Jesus. It is considered a Holy day for us and a very important day to go to the beach, weather we have money for a big feast or just enough to have a banana, rice and some dried fish to take along. Any amount of food is O.K. What is most important is to get wet and to enjoy the day together.

Until recent years, Filipinos did not observe Halloween in any way similar to Americans. All Saints Day, on November 1, is a day Filipinos pay homage to their dead. On that day we all go to the cemeteries to honor our deceased relatives. We take plates of food, flowers—in bunches and in wreaths—and candles, and place them on the graves for the dead. Churches are opened all day until late at night for those who wish to light candles to honor their deceased loved ones or to say prayers. Plates of the deceased's favorite food are placed on the tombs in the belief that their spirits visit the earth on this day and look forward to the special meal. The cemetery is prepared days in advance by having the tombs whitewashed or painted, the grass trimmed and incense left burning to give the site a fragrant smell, and a priest goes around and blesses and sprinkles holy water on the graves.

Today, in addition to all of this, because of increased Western influence, many Filipino adults and children now dress up in costumes and have neighborhood Halloween parties and costume-judging contests similar to those in the USA and other countries. Overall, it is mostly those who are financially well-off or who are doing it for the fun of the children. Also, in the Philippines it is fast becoming a favorite holiday for the gays who are now using it for a dress-up celebration to show off their *bonga* gowns and to compete in Gay Beauty contests.

For over ten years of my life in America now, I have noticed that American and Filipinos are having so much more in common. In the Philippines we have so many events and festivities that bring our people together almost every month and more and more of these observances are being influenced by American—or western—ways. In fact, it has often been said that the culture of the Philippines has always been about twenty or so years behind the U.S.A. Since I have been in America, I have learned that Filipino children now often call the police to complain about being spanked or run away from home after being disciplined—events unheard of in my day—and that lawsuits for nearly any kind of minor grievance are being filed much more often. I guess the future is destined to be the same the world over.

CHAPTER 13

The Filipino-American Culture

I wasn't sure if I really wanted to write my life story because I didn't think it was worth it. I knew I had not accomplished any great deeds or had ever done as much as some others and I knew that my education would always be in question. About all I had ever accomplished was work unremarkable, mundane jobs—which no one would think was so great—and perhaps I would only raise a lot of eyebrows of people of my country and with those in America with my courtship, marriage, and various other aspects of my domestic life. I'm pretty sure a majority of both countries probably don't necessarily like, nor are proud, of my doings. None of it is good enough to make them proud in my country, and maybe I give shame to some of them. But after deeply thinking about my life I decided I really did have a good story, not because I had overcome obstacles in my life to become a great doctor or surgeon or some sort of person like that, but because I had taken a chance and met a nice guy and had gotten out of poverty to make a better life for myself and for my entire family. In fact, I have been able to help spread my good fortune beyond my parents to help out my brothers and sisters and even my nephews and nieces. Today, I could go on to college and have even checked into it but I have chosen to wait for the sake of the young ones—my nephews and nieces—to finish. My husband and I are not rich but we are fortunate enough to stretch what we do have beyond ourselves to help out my parents each month, to provide vocational training for my brothers, to provide the occasional special needs for my sisters and their families—even to provide them land to live on to prevent them having to pay a monthly rent—and the schooling and special needs of the little ones. Perhaps some of the people of my country and a majority of Americans don't think much about what I have accomplished with my life, but I know a real big family in the Philippines who is extremely happy and thankful for it and I know that my Mother and Father are very proud of me. As for the Americans, most of them have no concept of what poverty *really* is or what it's like to be hungry and unable to get enough food. They don't know what it's like to be sick and need medicine or need an operation and be unable to afford neither and they have no concept of how you just do without, having no insurance coverage or no credit card, and you don't *somehow* come up with the money, you just lay there and let nature take its course. You let God decide if you will live or die.

Some Filipinos now in America are embarrassed or ashamed to talk about their past, the poverty of their families, the conditions of the homes they grew up in, and the difficulties they have gone through just to get to this country in order to have a better life and to help provide for their families. Some of my friends have encouraged me to complete this book while a majority have told me not to be so truthful because people will lose respect for many of us or will make fun of me or think less of me. But I think it is important that many Americans see just how fortunate they are to be here. That what they have and what they take for granted or sometimes are so quick to complain about, is not available to a majority of the people in this world, especially to those in the "third world," who are envious even of the poorest people of America. During our wedding reception one of my Aunts walked up to my husband and asked him, "Are you rich?" to which my husband smiled and responded, "No, I'm just an average American." My Aunt then asked, "Do you have a job?" and he answered "yes." She asked "do you own a car?" and he said "yes" and she then asked "do you have a place to live?" and he answered "yes" and then she frowned. As she turned to walk away, she smiled approvingly and said "Then Lonnie, by our standards, you are rich."

In addition to being shocked at the size of the food portions served in America, I was surprised at the lack of customer service provided in America and how rude consumers are sometimes treated compared to the Philippines. Perhaps we are more poor and less fortunate but in the Asian culture we go out of our way to be helpful or provide good service. In the department stores of our malls, it is not uncommon to have five to six salesgirls helping a customer try on clothing or retrieving additional sizes or colors off the rack for the consumer to try. My husband was amazed at the service he received one time while simply buying batteries for his camera. After choosing the size he needed, the salesgirl popped open the blister-wrap covering and placed the item in a battery-tester on the counter to show him the battery was fully charged and then resealed the wrap before bagging the item. This kind of attention and service is common in my country.

The attitude of the employer is different in America too. In the Philippines a company does not arbitrarily hand out applications. They must be purchased independently. In America, on the other hand, applicants can go around and apply at various companies without any cost or obligation. While in the Philippines we are just happy to have any paying job and often remain there as a devoted employee, Americans are often busy applying for better-paying jobs and seldom feel obligated to an employer. At the same time, I have noticed a strange competition going on between almost any company in America and its employees. I think it's rather humorous, but I have always noticed in the USA all the companies are constantly trying to convince the employees that it is doing them a favor by providing them a job while at the same time the employee's attitude is that they are doing the company a favor by working for them.

What is good, however, is the use of credit cards when one is short on cash. America makes it easier to preserve pride. In my country we have to go to a relative, a friend or someone wealthy in the neighborhood who generally makes loans available, and ask to borrow money for necessities or needs, sometimes. In the USA, on the other hand, we are able to prevent embarrassment or preserve our integrity by simply using a credit card. We don't have to face our creditor and swallow our pride to ask for credit—preserving *hiya*, our Asian pride!.

Another difference between American and Filipino customs involves the family obligations. I like in America that the children are raised to be independent of the parents with no absolute obligation to them. American children are raised from infancy in autonomy. Unlike the Philippines, American children are brought up in preparation to eventually go off and live their own life with their own families. Filipino parents regard the desire of their married children to live on their own or away from them as an indication of their unhappiness or as a lack of harmony within the family. In America, the child grows up and leaves home to get a job in order to support their own lifestyle and to lighten their parents' burden. In the Philippines a child goes off to get a job not only to help support the parents but also to help support all the remaining brothers and sisters. American children are not so much obligated to live near their parents or to take care of them and to provide for them financially as the children are in the Philippines. But in my country there are no nursing homes or retirement homes. It is considered a sacred obligation to provide for and care for one's parents. Not to do so would reflect badly on the child and would be looked upon as shameful. Their child would be regarded by others as bad, unappreciative and not loving of their parents.

Probably even more significant is the attitude differences between my country and America in raising the children. In America the children are constantly encouraged that they can be whatever they want to be or do whatever they love and enjoy when they grow up. They are raised with the belief that there are no limits to their life-long ambitions or interests. As I was growing up, no one gave me the opportunity to practice my singing and dancing purely for the sake of enjoyment. I was never encouraged to get proper training for it as I got older to try and make a profession out of it if I wanted to or thought I could. Basically then, Filipinos are person-oriented and raised as babies to be rich in love and devotion to their families while Americans are goal-oriented and raised as babies to become independent. Filipinos are raised to not rock the boat and to maintain the "status-quo" while Americans emphasize challenge, rebellion or "doing" and getting things done.

There are differences in other aspects too. In America the emphasis on women seems to be on their independence outside the home. My mom was never as fancy as other moms. As I explained, she only finished the Third grade. She had no knowledge of any history, physics or science and she never had any high degree that a person might achieve in those fields. But I think she had a higher score in PG—or parental guidance—than many of those other people. She was "top notch" in raising healthy babies, in cleanliness, in cooking, and as a good roll model as a strong women for all of us girls. To the people who know her—including our neighbors, our friends, her business associates, her customers, even strangers and of coarse our relatives—she is a good-hearted person. As long as she can afford it—sometimes even when she can't, on credit—she is willing to provide the whole village food or part of a good meal. She will share all of what she has or what she can with anyone. That is how she is. She can not stand to see a person that might be hungry without giving them food. She might even chew on a bone or do with less on her own plate in order to provide her family or her friends enough to eat. I have seen her do this with my own eyes. I have actually watched her chew and suck on a bone during our meal in order for us kids to have enough meat on our own plates.

We often had a *salo-salo*, or a little gathering, in our yard as a result of her having a good day in town, because she had sold a lot of fish or shrimp at the farmers market earlier that morning. Mama would always bring back fresh noodles, a kilo or two of pork, a packet of beef bones with traces of meat attached, and lots and lots of fresh vegetables. It seems neighbors, friends, and relatives would often come by as they smelled food being cooked over the open fire and begin a conversation in the hope they would be invited to stay for dinner. I remember my Uncle Nelson always coming by and as he talked to my mother he would drift over to the fire and eventually lift the lid to see what was cooking. If he liked what he saw, he would continue to hang around talking until it was meal-time. On those mornings Mama came home from the market with a lot of food, she and Papa would spend the rest of the day cooking and when it was all done they would distribute the food—one plate of noodles and a bowl of beef soup filled with vegetables—to any relatives who hadn't already come by. Mama would have me and Richein, and my other brothers and sisters run off in all directions to deliver the food to others in the neighborhood. The closest relatives received theirs first and then a few neighbors and others who often visited. Of course, simply the aroma of the food being cooked filtering through the neighborhood often drew friends, neighbors and relatives over to the yard to sit around and talk.

Perhaps my telling of the details about our lives or telling about my mom when I was a little girl through my teenage years might lead some to believe my mom was a menace or an abuser of her kids in American eyes, but my mama taught all of her kids to behave and to have respect for others. Now that I'm older and more mature, I know why she had to what she did. I also know I could never achieve what she did—the way she managed our family in all her strength. She made all of our meals everyday from scratch. She washed all of our clothes, cleaned all of the dishes, cleaned our house and everything she did was without the modern-day American conveniences or appliances but instead was by her hands. Yes, she delegated some of the work to us kids but that was part of her management abilities too. It wasn't to give her time to sit around. She helped Papa in his fishpond work in the time she saved having us kids do some of her housework. And during all of that she maintained a sideline of a little business store which helped out dad with our family expenses. In what spare time she could find, she used it to find fuel—firewood—for cooking. I do not know how she ever managed and divided all of her time to the various needs and duties. But I know that she did and that has always inspired me as well as my sisters. Mom taught us to be strong and take care of our home and family needs, no matter what little we have. She didn't need a college education and a degree to learn to become strong and independent and she taught that to each one of her daughters.

CHAPTER 14

The Changing Relationship With My Family

When I was 15-years old I competed in the annual Miss Timpolok beauty pageant held in our little barrio. My Uncle Fernando was a member of the Youth Organization that helped organize the event as part of the April celebration honoring our patron Virgin Mary or Mother of Perpetual Help that year.

For some reason, it was important to me to compete that year and my cousin Celia entered also. I guess we were just at that age when such things were of great significance in our lives but no one in my family would help me. My Mama told me it was a waste of our money and a waste of her time. There were various stages of the contest that involved competition in casual dresses, evening gowns, swimsuits and talent. I ran around and talked to all of my aunts and borrowed a dress from Antee Delia, a beautiful gown from Aunt Siding which she had received from her sister in-law from Germany, and a yellow swimsuit from Antee Tasing. All the dresses were very nice but just a little too big for me. Still, I was quite happy with them and it was so very nice of my aunts to loan them out to me. I was very grateful.

My talent was dancing and I did a nice little dance number. My sister Vilma and my brothers came to watch. Mama was right. I didn't win. Celia was very tall, with beautiful long legs, but she didn't win either. As usual, a girl with wealthy parents won the title Miss Timpolok that year. But winning didn't matter to me. I just wanted to try a real beauty pageant and see what it was like. Although I did not win that day I saw and heard all kinds of people who believed in me and enjoyed what I did on stage for my talent competition. And every time I walked across the stage I heard the crowd, drew their attention, and heard a lot of applause but I was sad that my mother didn't came to watch and that no one in my immediate family had wanted to help me prepare for it. It was supposed to be a fun event. Mama said it was a waste of time. She knew I wouldn't win. And she said that the competition was all baloney and full of crap presented by a bunch of shallow people. Perhaps she was right, but it was still a lot of fun and it would have been nice and pleased me a lot if she would have helped me participate. I guess she was just too busy at that time. Or perhaps she was just too embarrassed for us to be competing against the rich families of our community.

Much has changed since those numerous lectures I received from my mother. I send money every month to help with family expenses and my parents have become so proud of me. It wasn't long after I arrived in America that our neighborhood church arranged for our photographs to be taken for a new church directory—an event, by the way, that is unheard of in the Philippines. At my husband's suggestion, we purchased several additional framed 8X10 poses of me alone, in addition to one of us together, for my family. After the portraits arrived we sent them off to my parents and I later learned from my sister that when they were received, Papa was so proud that he cried as he took them around the neighborhood to show them off to everyone and then he and Mama mounted them on the walls of their home so they were immediately in view as anyone came through their front door. I understand both Mama and Papa proudly show them off to every visitor. "This is our daughter who lives in America," they proudly say.

After I had been married for a couple years and had moved away, my youngest brother announced to the family that he was Gay. He told me about it during one of my bi-weekly telephone calls. My papa and mama had both broke the news to me before Richein had taken his turn on the phone. My husband later informed me that he wasn't surprised. Lonnie claimed that he had always suspected Richein might be gay because, according to him, Richein had always acted somewhat feminine. And he saw no reason to mention it to me, he said, because it was purely speculation and it really didn't matter because Richein was a very sincere, respectful, well-mannered and well-behaved kid. In this day and age, Lonnie tried to explain, Richein's behavior and situation could be far worse. "Just let it go and accept it," he tried to tell me. But I couldn't. It mattered to me and it mattered a great deal! I was angry! Never mind what Richein might be going through. We were Catholic. My whole family was Catholic. And his revelation was against all that we had grown up with; against all that we had ever been taught in school or in church! And, I couldn't believe that my parents had accepted it! How could they? Why was happening in my country? What was wrong with everyone in the Philippines? Had they all lost their minds?

I was also upset with my mom for not cutting Richein's hair. "Perhaps that is what caused the problem," I started thinking! Now it was so hard to convince him to have a haircut like a man. He wanted longer hair and no one could convince him otherwise. When I got mad at Mom, she told me she had gotten old and it was difficult for her to see. She told me she hadn't noticed Richein's hair growing so long. I couldn't believe it! She had *never* given in that easily before.

At my insistence Mom and Dad told Richein to go somewhere for a haircut but he refused. At about the same time, my 14 year-old niece fell in love (or so she thought) and wanted to leave her parents, who were totally against the relationship, and move in to live with her boyfriend and his parents. Then her older brother Mecias, to whom Lonnie and I also contributed money to each month for his college tuition and expenses, ran away from home without telling anyone why or where he was going.

I was at a complete loss. I *thought* I had just started to make some differences in their lives. I had just begun to help them. What was happening to my family? What was wrong with everyone? Why was their world completely different from the world that I knew or had grown up to have? Family and religion—or even pride—was no longer as important to them as it was while I was growing up. What was happening to their lives? I only wish I could provide a definitive answer. Their world is different. Life, maybe because of TV, radio and computers, is faster now. Influences, both good and bad, are different today than when I was growing up too. The challenges are different and so are everyone's wants, wishes and needs. In recent years in the Philippines, religion and morals have declined while teen problems and out-of-wedlock pregnancies have increased. Separations and divorce, at one time unlawful in the Philippines, are now legal and increasing as well. And, like I said, it is now nearly unlawful to spank the children and so many more lawsuits are being filed in the country.

If the Philippines I grew up in was comparable to 1950s and early 1960s America—then the Philippines of today that they are growing up in is comparable to the America of the late 1970s to early 1980s.

My niece, Anebelle, moved out of her home, moved in with her boyfriend and several months later, due to complications, nearly died in childbirth. My parents helped pay her medical bills with the monthly expenses we provide until they could be reimbursed by her mother, my sister Helen who was then working abroad in Dubai, trying to get ahead in providing for her family. After several weeks, my nephew, Macias, returned home and announced that he had been accepted at the Saint Peter College Seminary in Butuan City, in the province of Agusan del Norte on Mindanao—a four-hour boat ride away from home—in preparation for the priesthood. We all knew he had wanted to be a priest since he was a child but he had gone on to the local college thinking that would please everyone in the family, especially Lonnie and me. Having no interest, however, we learned that he began flunking out after only half of his classes were completed and didn't know how to tell us so he ran away from home. He then went to the seminary, arranged for an interview and took the entrance exams to full-fill his life-long dream. Once accepted, he had regained enough pride to return home to announce his accomplishment to the family and to face the consequence of his running off.

In the midst of all of these "soap-operas" I have returned home to the Philippines twice during the past ten years that I have been married. Lonnie returned with me for the first return trip in 2001 after we had been married four years, to experience Easter in the Philippines. We had intended to return every four years after that but due to the ever-increasing costs of the flights, the second time I returned alone. We will return together in 2007, however, so Lonnie can experience Christmas in the Philippines. Eventually we hope to spend every December through February there once Lonnie is to able to retire.

Meanwhile, in March of 2003 I returned to the Philippines with several girl friends to visit my family through the middle of April. Four years had not passed since my previous visit but when this opportunity came up Lonnie advised I should go ahead and take advantage of it and we would postpone any 2005 trip unless we came into a lot of money!

The trip went well. This particular flight had a two-hour layover in Hong Kong which made a great shopping opportunity for us women. The Hong Kong International Airport is much like a big shopping mall so we made the best of it. But this was also the year that Severe Acute Respiratory Disease Syndrome (SARS) became a big scare and everyone—especially plane passengers with brief layovers—was required to wear surgical masks as they walked around the terminal. These were all passed out to the passengers as we debarked from our airplanes with instructions that they be worn as we remained at the airport. In addition, wherever we went or whatever we did was very limited at that time. After we departed, we then had to wear the mask the remainder of our trip into the Philippines because authorities there were also afraid that its citizens might be exposed to SARS. As we landed at the Cebu-Mactan International Airport, I was excited as we entered the terminal. I was looking forward to seeing my family but as we came down the escalator I noticed none of my relatives were anywhere around. As we all waited at the carousel for our luggage, I worried about where my family might be. When Lonnie and I had returned here a couple of years before, my family was waiting for us as we entered the building and approached the luggage carousels. This time, I now realized, I was in a different part of the terminal because I had come in on a different airline. I had arrived on Cathay Pacific airlines instead of PAL and their procedures were different. "This was not like my family," I worried, "not to be here waiting for me." I got my bags and stood around nervously beside the carousel looking all around while keeping an eye on my baggage.

"It's funny," I thought to myself, "but I had only been away from the Philippines for a few years and now I don't quite trust any of the strangers—my own countrymen—to be standing around my luggage for fear they might steal it." In that instance, I experienced feelings of being a foreigner in my own country. "So now," I thought, "I don't feel comfortable standing here by myself. Now I know what it feels like to be a foreigner in the Philippines. I don't feel like I am part of this country any more. I feel separated from all of these people."

I collected all my stuff. In addition to my luggage, I had shipped several large boxes—what we Filipinos call balik-bayan boxes—full of food and clothing for my family and I decided I should probably prepare for the worse. My bilik-bayan boxes—they weighed over 100-pounds each—had to be retrieved from another nearby carousel and placed on a cart so I could roll them out of the airport terminal and park them at the curb to await a taxi, if necessary. "I might have to arrange for transportation to my parents house or maybe my family was just late because of the heavy traffic," I thought to myself as I tried to calm down.

I was also anxious and nervous to see their faces and what they might look like after not seeing them for two years. The longer I waited, the more anxious I became. Again, I told myself I had to calm down. My family's absence really surprised me, though. I really expected to see them when I arrived and I really needed their help. In addition, their presence would make me feel a lot safer. In truth, I was scared without my family being here and getting all of these boxes and luggage items together for me and to get me good transportation out of here. I just didn't trust my countrymen. Especially those who seem to hang out around the airport. Its because some of them try to take advantage of the new arrivals and tourists by committing frauds, cheating them, or committing petty crimes. Those loitering around the airports are usually unreliable. So I loaded my luggage onto the cart with my boxes, realizing nobody was going to be coming for me. "You had better start taking care of yourself," I decided, "and quit standing around here." I was really becoming upset by now. I truly believed my family would be here to meet me, or at least one of them. "How could this happen!" I thought to myself as I pulled my cart toward the door. I was losing my patience, especially because I didn't know what was going on or what had happened to them.

I fell into line behind my friends when I noticed all them still in the area, slowly being processed through the terminal doors to the outside. In my country, there is a last stop security check for our carry-ons, luggage and boxes before we can leave the terminal completely to verify and make certain that all of the luggage and boxes that we are leaving with are actually ours.

As I stood there, a man came up offering to help me. I declined his offer. I wasn't about to let him or any stranger carry my belongings besides my family. I was afraid he might run off with it. But then I saw a badge or ID on his chest and noticed he was also wearing a uniform and decided that should be enough proof for me to perhaps trust him. "Huh!," I thought. "Maybe it's part of his job and if I refuse I might get in trouble." Then I saw my friend Jeanie, up ahead, let someone dressed like this help her, so I turned my cart over to him immediately. I was scared of being lost and scared of my own countrymen. It was pathetic, but I just didn't trust any of them.

When we finally arrived outside, my heart was pumping as fast as I could imagine. Again, I didn't see my family and I just didn't know for sure what I should do without them. "Should I wait in case they're on the way and running late or should I go on toward their home without them?" I wondered and worried. I just didn't trust getting any transportation on my own here. Perhaps I had just become accustomed to driving myself and had lost my ability to flag down and haggle over the carrier prices like I used to do. "I feel like a stranger in my own country," I kept worrying. "What if I get a taxi driver who takes advantage of my situation?"

As I found myself nearing the street near the front of the terminal, I found myself mumbling, "What happened? Why isn't my family here?" Then the man who was helping me with my luggage began telling me that his job was over because he couldn't walk out past the front gates. He told me this several times without me making a response before he finally just asked me for a tip for all of the help he had just provided. I was getting more nervous and upset. I didn't realize I was supposed to give him a tip for his help and I didn't have any idea of just how much to give. I also realized I hadn't exchanged any money inside the terminal and had no "pesos" with me. I quickly looked around and noticed most of my friends had already met up with their families outside but, lucky, Jeanie's family hadn't arrived yet either. She looked over at me from a distance but I think my face was hard to read or maybe too deformed to understand what my problem was. I was in a panic for a moment. I needed help. It was almost as if I was going to cry but I refused to drop any tears. All of a sudden my friend Genelyn came out of nowhere and asked if I needed help. I knew I was being pathetic, I was so innocent and naive about traveling without Lonnie. He had always taken care of everything, I was beginning to realize.

Genelyn had been off to one side, surrounded by her family but had noticed a strange look on my face and realized something was wrong. She asked me if I was alright so I told her what my problem was and she offered to loan me some money—peso bills—for a tip. I was relieved after paying the guy the amount of five hundred peso. "At least one problem solved," I thought to myself and smiled for a moment. Then I was back again worrying what went wrong with my family. I was praying and begging to the Lord that my family would show up and hoping they would have some spare money that I could use to pay my debt to Genelyn.

All of my friends offered to stay and wait with me or to give me a ride but I assured them I would be OK and that they should go ahead and leave with their families. I hadn't completely convinced myself I would be OK but I didn't want to be a bother to them.

Within a short time most of my friends and their families all got taxis and left. I stood there waiting and looking around for *my* family. I felt so all alone.

As I waited, I created a huge scene in my head arguing back and forth about why they weren't here and trying to convince myself I was safe and had no need to feel any fear. I kept praying too. All I asked was to see some sign of my family. I didn't care about anything else and I didn't care what their excuse was or how they would look. I just hopeed they were safe and on their way to find me.

Then I saw one of my brothers, Carlito. He was on the other side of the street some 30 yards away from me. He was walking along the sidewalk in a crowd of people. The sight of him was a sign just enough to relieve me and heal my mental illness that I think I had begun to create after waiting what I thought was a long period of time.

"Brod.! Brod.! I'm here! Brod. Carlito!" I called out. Finally, I caught his attention. He got a huge smile on his face. A very bright smile. "Manoy," he called back. "What happened?"

"Where is Mom and Dad?" I called out. But Carlito did not respond to me. Instead he turned and shouted down the street behind him, "Pa! Pa! Hurry! She's here." Then my father came running up to him, looked over across the street at me and ran to me as Carlito pointed me out. As Papa arrived at my side as Carlito ran to me from across the street.

"Pa?" I asked, "Where is Mom? Is she here?"

"Yes," he answered. "She's with Helen, Richein, Vilma and your nieces and nephews.

"I was mad at you guys," I confessed. "You take much too long to show up. Do you have any money I can use? I owe a friend some money."

"No," dad replied, "But your sister Helen brought some and she'll be along with your brothers and the others shortly."

I then learned that they had all waited for me at the Philippine Airlines gate where they had waited for me and Lonnie in the past. I had told them I was coming in on Cathay Pacific but it didn't occur to any of us that their arrival gate would be on the opposite end of the airport. Anyway, after they had waited for some time and saw no trace of me, they made an inquiry at the main information desk and found out that I had come in on another airline at another gate. Trying to get there, they learned they couldn't even get close because of security precautions set up since our first visit. Since the terrorist attack in America in 2001, people without plane tickets were no longer allowed in the terminal My family had no other choice but to patrol up and down the street hoping to see me come out of the terminal.

Within a short time my mom and the others arrived and surprised me with a sampaguita necklace.[7] I was embarrassed, especially in front of Genelyn who was still standing around nearby, "Who do you think I am," I said. "A president?" A graduate student?" But my complaint went unnoticed as we all began to cry and hug each other. They were happy to see me, they said, because they had worried so much about me on this trip due to the constant threat of terrorists, suicide bombers, and SARS.

I was relieved to see them, too. All of my family had come. Their faces were so different from my last visit. Papa and Mama were both thinner The little nephews and nieces were older. Richein was much taller. I couldn't help but wonder why they all looked like they'd had nothing to eat. "Where does the money go?" I thought to myself. Then all of my family had the same question about me and asked why I looked so skinny to their eyes. "Aren't you getting enough to eat?" my mom and sisters asked. "Yes," I answered. "But it's expected that we stay thin and fit in America." When I first arrived in the Philippines, I believed that so much had changed since I had been living in America, both with my country and with my family. Within days, however, I realized how much I had changed my own self! I remember as a teen going to the fish market with my mother. As she shopped and looked over what was available she would always send me over to one vendor who offered varieties of fresh salted seafood. In the booth was big plastic containers or kegs of salted shrimp, salted mussels, and salted little fish—two or three varieties about minnow size. I would walk up, point, and say "ten pesos ma'm" and the vendor would scoop up a certain amount from the container that I had pointed to and place the scooping in a plastic bag. Such was purchased for resale in Mama's store as well as for our own family's use. Although it is still sold like this today, now after living in America I worry about germs and sanitation. The same is true about eggs, sea food and meat sold in street markets. In the Philippines there are no regulations, no expiration dates. The people are so naive and innocent. They don't know to worry about such things!

On this trip I wished, at times, that I didn't know about such things either. I fretted as Mama and I walked and shopped around the fish market and circulated among the street vendors. I tried to explain such things to my mother but she acted as though she didn't understand until finally she stopped and said, "We buy the best we can here and take our chances. If we worry and buy nothing, we starve to death. Which do you prefer?"

Sometimes I miss being so naive and innocent. I think my life would be much more restful and relaxing not to know the dangers lurking around us. But it is now too late. I have learned American ways and American concerns. I cannot force my new beliefs and ways onto my family who must continue to live their lives here. Their daily concerns are different. They are not as worried about expiration dates on food, germs, or about being physically fit as I have become. It is something I have to constantly remind myself.

But, as I take my sisters to the malls and stores to shop, mama wants to go everywhere with me. Like a little child, she begins to cry when I tell her to stay home because I'm taking one of my sisters out to help with family needs. I found myself unable to have quality time alone with each of my sisters without feeling guilty about leaving Mama at home. We were able to get by with it a couple of times but, for the most part of this trip, Mama tagged along with us on all our shopping trips to pick out things she needed or wanted.

I have also been fortunate, since coming to America, to be able to purchase land for my brothers and sisters to build their little homes on so that they didn't have to pay rent for land elsewhere. They live on the property rent free so they can use that money for their other monthly family expenses. I have also helped my parents pay off the mortgage and debts for their land.

Eventually, Lonnie and I hope to buy our own acreage in the Philippines and build a nice home to live in during the USA's winter months. Of course, we also want to have enough land to create a little compound for my entire family to live in. That way they can watch over and take care of our home and all of my little nephews and nieces can be close enough to hang out at our home during the time we are living there.

As I mentioned earlier, my oldest sister Helen eventually went to work in far off Dubai. Because of a worsening economy in the Philippines Lorreto, her husband and father of Mecias, Annabel, J.R. and Lonnie Mark, was laid off from his lucrative welding job in early 2005. Frantically he tried to find similar work with other companies but none of them were hiring. For the next several months all he could find was temporary and short-term construction work. Helen took in wash, hired herself out for house-cleaning, and started a lunch counter at the front of her home in an effort to make ends meet. After a while, she began having health problems and after I and her family continued to insist that she go to a doctor, we learned she was suffering from stress. I sent additional expenses to my parents whenever possible as I knew they were helping Helen's family too. As her family's conditions were growing desperate, Helen asked me if I could help her get a passport and other government forms and papers and she further advised me that she would reimburse me for any expenses incurred as she sought employment outside the Philippines. Her request surprised me but I agreed to do all I could.

On September 9, 2005 Helen said goodbye to her family, our siblings and our parents as she prepared to leave the Philippines. A few weeks before, she had been chosen by a family living in the Mid-East through her sponsorship company for employment as a domestic helper. She was heading out for the other side of the world to live in a country and in a culture she knew nothing about except for what she had read or seen on TV. She was chosen to work for a wealthy family in Dubai, in the United Arab Emirates.

This was something she never would have considered before. But since I had gotten married and had left the country to seek a better life, my adventure and my good fortune had inspired her in some ways and made her brave. Because of the poor economy, Lorreto remained unable to find another decent job. With their

Mirror of My Past

two oldest children entering high school and the two others ready to enter grade school, Helen and Lorreto reluctantly decided it was best that one of them find employment wherever necessary. An employment agency in Cebu City found a high-paying housekeeper position for Helen with the wealthy family in the U.A.E. The company would pay for her air fare and other expenses and would then be reimbursed out of Helen's first few paychecks as long as she agreed in writing to continue in the employment for 24 months. After much discussion and planning with her family, she accepted the position. Before she left she had called me to say goodbye. She had never been on an airplane. She had never been away from Cebu or her family. Her first words was asking me if I wanted her to go or stay and my reply was simply to tell her, "Sorry, it is your decision. Its like me marrying a foreigner. Only I could decide that, on my own." Then she laughed and said she was just kidding, she had already realized that and had made already made the decision. "Besides" she said, "if I decide not to go now, I would have to face a huge problem. I would be black-listed with the company which means I could not go anywhere and the plane ticket and all the paperwork that had been processed would still have to be paid." There was no backing out now!

We talked for quite some time. She was excited but scared and wasn't sure what to expect once she arrived. We both cried as we talked. I told her to write and give me her address and phone number as soon as possible and I would call so we could then stay in touch like we did when she was in the Philippines. She agreed and soon boarded her plane.

After nearly three months I received her first letter with a telephone number to call. Before I could comply, her boss called me and put her on the phone. Helen was with a nice family. The gentleman owned a big shoe company and the Misses encouraged Helen to call me and stay in touch and, in fact, had helped her place the call. Helen was now quite happy and confident. Once she arrived there and got settled, she became comfortable and developed a routine. We now talk as often as before, about every three weeks or so. Her room and board is provided so she sends nearly all of her salary home to her family. She has since provided them with a computer hooked up to the Internet and all the other modern conveniences a family of today needs. Her oldest son, Meceias, my nephew, has also become more confident and independent. I like to think that he, too, has been influenced by me and his mother and has gone on to realize *his* dreams. He is hard at work making his dream of becoming a priest in the Catholic church a reality. After being tested and passing all of the exams in May and June of 2006, he was accepted for the priesthood and will be eventually going to Rome where he will remain studying and working in the Vatican.

With financial help from me and Lonnie, my brother Carlito was able to finish his high school education and additional technical training in automobile mechanics. He studied hard—which was difficult for him after being out of school for so long—and proudly graduated. He is now seeking employment in that field and has so much more confidence in himself and his own abilities.

My little brother Richein eventually got a job in the medical field, several months after Lonnie and I had provided the money for his medical training and additional education and we also help my other brother, Ferdinand, whenever we can with additional expenses that come up with his family and his children's needs.

In addition, I help Vilma and her family too, as the need arises and, as with Ferdinand, provide money and clothing for their children—all of my many little nephews and nieces—whenever I can. Lonnie and I eventually helped Vilma realize her life-long dream of traveling to Korea to work. We helped her with her tuition in training and Korean language lessons in June of 2006 and she is now on a waiting list for a position opening there. All of us girls have already decided that every four years we will all meet back in the Philippines for a family reunion and will continue to do so no matter where or in what country we all work and live.

I have continued to stay in touch with many of my nephews and nieces now in the computer "chat rooms" But their world has become so different than the world I had—the world I grew up in. Although many of their needs are the same that I once had, they all have many more needs that are different and I wish that I had the answer to all of their problems. Sometimes their problems and complaints make me laugh out loud—or LOL as we refer to it in the "chat rooms"—but I wish that they could all have the life that I have. I wish that I could afford to give them all the life that they need or even let them live my life for me. Sometimes it doesn't seem fair. There are so many in my country—in the world, for that matter—that deserve so much better. I guess we will never have all the answers. I think the trials and errors in our lives help many of us reach our goals of happiness and help direct our constant strive toward perfection. For many it helps build character. Without experiencing one, we often will never know the other.

I know that my Papa's mama, Grandma Gregoria, was proud of me. She had come to visit and stay with us when I returned to visit my family in March of 2003. Lola Gregoria and I talked as I combed her hair and she told me quite frankly that she was proud of me and happy for me and for what my life had become. Sadly, she passed away several months after I returned home to the USA after that trip but I was happy that we had spent so much time together and talked so freely before she had passed away.

Since then I call my family nearly every week some months and sometimes several times a week if necessary. Other times we talk in the "chat rooms" with one of my nephews or nieces as the rest of my Philippines family gather around the computer to join in on the conversation. Even my brother Richein chats with me or Lonnie on the computer from various cyber cafes throughout Lapu-Lapu or Cebu City on nearly a weekly basis. Like my Uncle Fernando, Richein has a number of pen-pals throughout the world—but he stays in touch with them on a weekly or sometimes nightly basis via computer.

As I look back I worry about Richein. His situation makes me angry but I can't help but worry about him. It makes me think back about my Uncle Fernando and how much I loved him. He was the all-time master of ceremonies and entertainment director for our barrio. The older people all seemed to like him and his work. As I look back and reminisce about my childhood days through my teenage years, I realize he was indeed my dearest uncle if not my very best uncle of all. Like my grandpa, Fernando was also very popular but in different ways. My first memories of him was when I was in the first grade. I guess that would make my first memories be when I was six years old and Fernando was already a teenager. I remember how some people mistreated him and even at six and seven years old I didn't understand it. I didn't understand how they could mistreat and be so mean to such a soft-spoken, fun loving, gentle and kind individual. And then his death came. I remember that day so vividly. Uncle Fernando's death was a family mystery. Someone discovered his body floating in the water beneath the bridge that led into Cebu City. People, perhaps it was the police, brought his body to the Lapu-Lapu Funeral home and notified our family. Then they informed us that someone in the family had to come see if they could recognize and identify the body. Mama went along with her brothers. The body was wearing a Pentax t-shirt that Uncle Fernando had once borrowed from Vilma. Inside the pocket of the t-shirt was a rosary that Uncle Fernando had owned and with the body was a piece of underwear or swim wear that Uncle Fernando had once borrowed from other relatives. This was all that could be used to identify poor Uncle Fernando. His body, his face, was unrecognizable. He had been floating in the ocean water for three days and was badly swollen. At the funeral they tried the best they could to preserve the body but no matter what they did the body was just too deteriorated. I felt so sorry for Uncle Fernando. It just wasn't fair! Even in death, it seemed, he was being mistreated. He had always been so nice to everyone but even after dying he couldn't even receive a normal funeral. It is still so hard to believe he died. It was so hard to accept. Because of his condition he was covered up so we could not see him. And it gave me the opportunity to believe it was not really him. "He just went abroad to another country to be with one of his penpals," I wanted to believe. But when months and years came and went and yet he still didn't show up, I was convinced that it must have been him. I miss him so much. I notice, too, that his brothers and sisters who had once spoke so ill of him have always been sad and regretted their lack of love for him when he was alive. They realize how much they miss him now. Why do we always wait until it is too late?

I didn't want that to happen to Uncle Fernando. I wouldn't want that to happen to anyone. It's hard to imagine what I might have thought of him had I known the truth about Uncle Fernando. It is difficult to believe I could have thought of him any differently.

And as it was with the knowledge about Uncle Fernando, eventually—although I still don't agree with the lifestyle—I am able to get past the idea of my brother being Gay. Richein is my little brother and I love him. Even though *he* wishes he was my little sister—I still love him!

In my own life, I now own a dress shop and boutique in a small tourist town near the Blue Ridge Mountains in North Carolina. With Lonnie's help, I am a successful business owner and entrepreneur and I am in the process of getting American citizenship. Perhaps I will eventually be able to get my brothers here to help me—after all, Richein knows a lot about fashion—and get my parents here to visit. The future looks wonderful and I am very happy.

So, sometimes it works to become brave and leave your own people to seek what is not there or what you cannot find. Sometimes it works to get away from the people who ridicule you for having a dream that they gave up on, or lost site of, a long ago. It might not work for everyone but it worked for me. I have found so much! So much more than I could ever ask for. I have found love. I have found confidence in myself. I have found beauty within myself. And I have found pride and happiness that has remained unequaled.

I guess a person's life is much like the plants we use in landscaping. Like in gardening, some plants won't survive in certain soils or in certain locations with limited lighting. To put it simply, for a variety of reasons, some just thrive better in one place than another—and some look better in one location than they do in another. So, the way I plant mine is keep trying until I find the right place and the right environment.

Endnotes

Prologue

1. Teodoro A. Agoncillo, *History of the Filipino People* (Quezon City: Garotech Publishing,1990), p. 20-29.

2. Antonio Pigafetta, R. A. Skelton, trans., *Magellan's Voyage, A Narrative Account of the first Circumnavigation* (New Haven, CT: Yale University Press, 1969), p. 87-88, hereafter referred to as Pigafetta, *Magellan's Voyage.*

3. Lonnie R. Speer, "Death of Magellan: Ferdinand Magellan's overconfidence in technology prevented him from circumnavigating the world," *Military History*, Vol. 18, No. 5 (Dec. 2001); Lonnie R. Speer, "Where Magellan Met his Maker," *Filipinas*, April 2002.

4. Pigafetta, *Magellan's Voyage*, p. 84-88.

5. Ibid.

6. Ibid., p. 87-88.

7. Ibid.; Charles M. Parr, *So Noble A Captain* (NY: Thomas Y. Crowell, 1953), p. 347-362; Ian Cameron, *Magellan* (NY: Saturday Review Press, 1973), p. 180-192; Tim Joyner, *Magellan* (Camden, ME: International Marine, 1992), p. 191-197.

8. Ibid.

9. Jens Peters, *Philippines* (Berkeley, CA: Lonely Planet Publications, 1991), p. 26; Dirk J. Barreveld, *Philippines in a Nutshell* (Mandaue City, P.I.: Arcilla Travel Guide Publishing, 2000), p. 10; Sylvia Mayuga and Alfred Yuson, *Philippines* (Boston: Houghton Mifflin, 2000), p. 81; Ferdinand E. Marcos, *The New Philippine Republic* (Manila, P.I.: n. p., 1982), p. 2-15; Stanley Karnow, *In Our Image, America's Empire in the Philippines* (NY: Random House, 1989), p. 444-445.

10. Sylvia Mayuga and Alfred Yuson, *Philippines* (Boston: Houghton Mifflin, 2000), p. 81-83.

11. Dirk J. Barreveld, *Philippines in a Nutshell* (Mandaue City, P.I.: Arcilla Travel Guide Publishing, 2000), p. 10; Maria E. Paterno, *Volcanoes of the Philippines* (Manila: Tahanan Books, 1992), p. 4, 15-16; Maria E. Paterno, *Typhoon!* (Manila: Tahanan Books, 1993), p. 18-21.

12. Henry R. Wagners, "Unamuno's Voyage to California in 1587," *Quarterly of California Historical Society*, (July 1923); Lorraine Jacobs Crouchett, *Filipinos in California* (1982); Fred Cordova, *Filipinos: Forgotten Asia Americans* (Dubuque,

IA: Kendall/Hunt Publishing, 1983), p. 1-20; Veltisezar Bautista, *The Filipino Americans, From 1763 to the Present* (Farmington Hills, MI: Bookhaus Publishers, 1998), p. 5, 11-18.

13. Arthur Zich, "Hope and Danger in the Philippines," *National Geographic* (July 1986), p. 92-115; Isabelo T. Crisostomo, *Filipino Achievers in the USA & Canada* ((Farmington Hills, MI: Bookhaus Publishers, 1996), p. 1-6, 19-25; I. N. S., U.S. Department of Justice, 1998 Statistical Yearbook of the Immigration and Naturalization Service (Washington, DC: GPO, 2000).

Chapter 1

1. Opon was the original name of Lapu-Lapu City. The town was renamed in 1961 to honor the country's "first national hero." Although Cebu City is the country's oldest community, it ranks only third in size and population. It is located 350 miles, about an hour flight, south of Manila.

2. Lola is our word for grandmother and Lolo is our word for grandfather.

3. There are about 100 species of lizards in the Philippines, none of which are poisonous. The most familiar is the "house lizard" or gecko, whose feet have tiny little suction cups that enable it to scurry along the ceilings and walls in its night-long search for mosquitoes, flies and roaches. The geckos will range anywhere from about an inch to five inches long. The "tu-ko," so-named for its bird-like call, average about a foot in length and normally live in trees around the house. They, too, feed on insects. House lizards are considered good luck in the Philippines. Having a large "tu-ko" in the house is considered unbelievably lucky.

4. The adults used this creature to scare the children into staying around the house and not to wander off out of sight to play, etc. Apparently a number of children in the community had fallen victim to a child molester, never to be seen again, and it was much easier to scare them with a creature than to try and explain about child molestation and murder.

Chapter 2

1. Even with the alternatives of today, my parents still prefer to obtain a majority of their food items shortly before they plan to prepare the meal, strongly believing that frozen foods are not as healthy, taste differently, and are not as palatable.

2. As I look back, perhaps Mama was also afraid Grandpa would have made too many demands for his financial help.

3. *Lubi* is the word for coconut in the Visayan dialect.

4. There is no kindergarten in the Philippines. We begin our schooling, in the "first grade."

5. I guess my upset and worries was from my *hiya*—another test of my pride.

Chapter 5

1. The land was sold and passed through several hands. Shortly after I was married new homes and condominiums were built all across the site. My husband later talked of the possibility of acquiring one of the condominiums but was persuaded by Papa to look elsewhere because the filled-in fish ponds throughout the area were still causing settling problems with many of the homes.

2. Apparently I hadn't found all of it. A few years after I was married, Papa sent my husband a handful of old collectible Filipino coins, some very rare, that he had found hidden throughout the house over the past few years and said he wanted my husband to have them.

Chapter 6

1. Since having dispensed with their publications, the services that still exist now use web-sites on the computer internet.

2. Generally, flowers were ordered through various companies in the USA which then arranged for them to be purchased locally in the Philippines for delivery.

3. Bogart: A slang expression used by many Filipinos to mean "a boastful tough-acting American" much like the characters Humphry Bogart played in the 1940s and 1950s American movies.

4. Not until I arrived in America did I become comfortable around cats and began to like them. Still, I prefer white cats with green eyes over black cats with yellow eyes.

Chapter 7

1. Based on the works of Filipino psychiatrist Lourdes V. Lapus, and his book *A Study of Psychopathology.*

2. Ibid.

3. Ibid.

4. Although the word "Filipino" refers to any male or female citizen of the Philippines, the word "Filipina" is a term referring strictly to the female Filipino.

Chapter 8

1. I never knew if Grandpa meant it or not but it didn't really matter, it made me feel good. *Put-Put-Put* was a reference to her flatulence—or uncontrollable release of gas whenever she got excited.

2. I later asked Lonnie about this but he maintained he never sent anyone or paid for any pen-pal service to do a background investigation on me. We all later speculated that some other pen-pal might have had someone sent or the stranger was, himself,

one of my former pen-pals trying to locate me or my house. Our homes do not have house numbers. Everyone, including the post people, simply know who lives in each house or uses the same method of questioning those in the neighborhood when trying to locate someone in particular.

3. Grandma Eutropia Tumulak passed away in March 1997—a month after our wedding—after I had come to America. I like to think that although she hadn't been able to speak, she had been able to see Lonnie and know that I had a wonderful wedding and had fulfilled her husband's dream of going to America before she passed away.

Chapter 9

1. Strangely, it is a twelve-and-a-half hour flight from LA to Manila because the plane is flying westward into the headwinds. The flight eastbound, *with* the wind, averages about one-and-a-half hours less.

2. Unfortunately, it took a while for it all to sank in with me. Every time he had explained something like this in a letter, my family just thought he was being cheap or some kind of a great pretender who was wanting to test me to see if I was looking for his fortune. They had me convinced of that. It really didn't matter to me anyway so I didn't pay too much attention to it when he tried to explain about money in America and how hard we had to work in order to get it, what it took in America to have it, or the cost of living in this country. I was originally too busy believing that everyone in America was rich and I had little knowledge of any other country's lifestyle or cost of living. For instance, I didn't realize having our own car was a necessity in America and then was confronted with the cost of insurance for that car, license and tax expenses on that car, the weekly fuel expense for that car, costs of repairs and upkeep for that car, and so on. I had been blind to it all and never fully understood until I had lived here for a while and had helped work for what we had. Then the reality of it hit me hard right in my face!

Chapter 10

1. By the year 2000, chocolates and fresh milk became more easily available and common place in the Philippines and are now as commonly available as it is in the United States.

Chapter 11

1. The following year, 1999, Lonnie and our friends entered me in the association's annual Mrs. Valentine contest and I was fortunate enough to win.

2. Currently a Philippine peso is equal to about two-cents in US currency.

3. The American Automobile Association (AAA) offers emergency help and "Roadside Assistance" for an annual fee.

4. Several months later we read that this same man had lost his job for this kind of behavior and that there had been additional complaints before our dealings with him.

5. Much like the economy of Mexico, according to the latest statistics available, 56 per-cent of the $8.5 billion or about $4.76 billion sent to the Philippines in 2004 originated from the United States (*Filipinas*, October 2006, p.3).

Chapter 12

1. Saint Peter and Saint Paul. The feast day commemorates the martyrdom of these two great apostles.

Chapter 14

1. A Sampaguita necklace is what Americans would call a Lei. The Sampaguita is the National flower of the Philippines and such Leis are normally presented by the President of our country to visiting dignitaries. Mother thought she was doing something special—giving me a great honor by presenting me with the beautiful fresh flower Lei, but I found it terribly embarrassing.